MODERN
ULSTER
ARCHITECTURE

Ulster Museum Extension

DAVID
EVANS

MARK
HACKETT

ALASTAIR
HALL

PAUL
LARMOUR

CHARLES
RATTRAY

MODERN ULSTER ARCHITECTURE

UAHS

Belfast 2006
A publication of
the Ulster
Architectural
Heritage Society

First published 2006 by
the Ulster Architectural Heritage Society
66 Donegall Pass, Belfast BT7 1BU

©UAHS & D.Evans, M.Hackett, A.Hall,
P.Larmour and C.Rattray

Editor   Karen Latimer
Design Fishbone Studio Ltd
Print   Graham & Heslip

Hardback
ISBN-10 0-900457-66-X
ISBN-13 978-0-900457-66-1

Paperback
ISBN-10 0-900457-67-8
ISBN-13 978-0-900457-67-8

A CIP catalogue record for this book is
available from the British Library.

Supported by
The National Lottery®
through the Arts Council of Northern Ireland
arts council of Northern Ireland
UAHS

Acknowledgements

The authors would like to acknowledge the support of the UAHS whose experience and resources have been fundamental to the completion of the project. Particularly we would like to thank Peter Marlow for his patient project management and, especially, Karen Latimer for bearing the brunt of the editorial and administrative burden whilst providing such welcome encouragement to all of us during a period that was not without its difficulties and pressures.

The authors would also like to acknowledge with thanks the help of the architects of the buildings and projects featured as case studies in Parts Two and Three. In addition, for photographs or drawings which they have contributed or for other information, the authors would like to thank MAGNI, Paul Millar and Joe Tracey. John Lawlor, Nigel Murray, Francis Peel and Domenika Placek carried out excellent work on the drawings for the McCormick churches, the Ulster Museum, the Ashby Institute and the Ardhowen Theatre respectively. Our thanks are also due to Scadin for their assistance with the preparation of various drawings.

The UAHS would like to acknowledge with gratitude the generous financial assistance towards the publication of this book of the Arts Council of Northern Ireland, Primrose and Edward Wilson, Ulster Garden Villages and the Esme Mitchell Trust.

Conventions

The initials of the author of each building study are given at the end of the text.

David Evans	DE
Alastair Hall	AH
Paul Larmour	PL

0 └──────┘ 10

All measurements are in metres

CONTENTS

FOREWORD

The Ulster Architectural Heritage Society is proud to publish this book on modern Ulster architecture. It follows on from David Evans's 1977 pioneering study, *An Introduction to Modern Ulster Architecture*, also published by the Society. Appropriately David is a major contributor to this book and the Arts Council of Northern Ireland has again provided significant funding. The UAHS is pleased to have taken on the publication of a book originally mooted by the Royal Society of Ulster Architects some time ago. We are grateful to the RSUA for supporting the project.

The authors are David Evans, Alastair Hall, Paul Larmour and Charles Rattray, with Mark Hackett taking, or sourcing, many of the photographs. Karen Latimer's editorial skills have been effectively applied to the entire manuscript while Sam Bell of Fishbone Studio has designed and managed the production of the book. Peter Marlow, as Chairman of the UAHS, managed the project. To all of them the Society is deeply grateful.

No such selection of some fifty buildings from hundreds to choose from can please everyone. We all, professional architects, architectural historians, academics and interested amateurs, will question why one was included and another omitted. We welcome that debate. The final selection was agreed by the team jointly but the Ulster Architectural Heritage Society accepts full responsibility for the final decisions.

The book is intended to provide an overview of recent architecture in Ulster to the widest possible audience. Architectural practices will take pride in the quality of work that has been produced in recent years; students of all ages and disciplines will learn much from the buildings described here and from the underpinning essays; those with a general interest in architecture, both locals and those from further afield, can see what a positive image modern architecture in Ulster projects and, we hope, come to see many of the buildings for themselves. This is a beautiful book written by knowledgeable people about good buildings in a community to which we are all committed. We want to share it with as broad an audience as possible.

Peter O. Marlow
CHAIRMAN UAHS 1999-2006

The Arts Council of Northern Ireland has provided National Lottery funding through its Architecture Special Initiative for the publication of the book. The Arts Council seeks to encourage greater appreciation of architecture as an artistic and cultural enterprise, and to promote wider and deeper critical debate about Northern Ireland's built environment. In providing the grant to the UAHS in order to develop – wholly independently – this landmark publication we believe that further informed discussion can and will take place. In addition to the main funding the UAHS received grants from Ulster Garden Villages, the Esme Mitchell Trust and from Primrose and Edward Wilson. Without their support this book could not have been produced.

Paul Harron
ARTS DEVELOPMENT MANAGER
(ARCHITECTURE AND PUBLIC
REALM SPECIALIST) ARTS COUNCIL
OF NORTHERN IRELAND

Mervyn Black
PRESIDENT RSUA 2004-6

INTRODUCTIC

In a general sense 'modern architecture' is an imprecise term traditionally used to describe the present state of architectural evolution and meaning anything from current architecture, or architecture of the present day, to architecture of the 'modern' period, that period meaning anything from the late 18th to the late 20th centuries, and embracing all buildings regardless of their ideological basis. In a narrower sense, however, the term 'modern architecture' has been used during much of the last century to refer specifically to an architecture which is, in the words of one historian, 'conscious of its own modernity and striving for change.'¹ This type of architecture was born early in the 20th century in reaction to what seemed to some to be the excessive historicism of the 19th century, and was spurred on by a combination of the potential of new materials and technical processes. It was inspired by the exciting structural and spatial opportunities offered by the new materials of glass, reinforced concrete and steel and also the idealistic belief that the new and better world needed new forms of architectural expression. It is this more particular sense that defines the subject of our book.

Modern Architecture in Ulster is set out in three parts – thematic and chronological essays of which there are three, an extensive series of individual building studies and a number of, as yet, unbuilt projects. In Part One the first essay deals with the search for the modern in local architecture in the period 1900 to 1950, telling the story of the early Modern Movement in Ulster as seen against a largely historical revivalist background. The second essay traces the later flowering of this movement from 1950 onwards to culminate in what we can see to be the mainstream development in contemporary

architecture in Ulster. The third essay offers an overview of recent architecture in Ulster set in the context of progressive Modernism internationally.

In Parts Two and Three the individual building studies and projects present the second half of the 20th century and the first few years of the 21st in a series of detailed examples. These are very selective for the earlier decades, chosen to illustrate the particular preoccupations of the time with either the best surviving examples or at least those which retain as much of their original integrity as could be hoped for, but increase in number the nearer we reach the present day so as to give a wide-ranging picture of current modern architecture in Ulster. What we refer to here as 'modern architecture' is still an enduring concept, although it has been challenged comparatively recently by the idea of Postmodernism. Postmodernism is itself, of course, obsessed with the idea of 'modernity', which brings us back to the starting premise of the book.

The choice of buildings in this series of case studies is highly subjective, and personal to each of the contributing authors to some degree. While some of the buildings can be regarded as 'classics', and as such will probably not be disputed, the inclusion of others will undoubtedly raise the question of many more omissions. Some award-winning buildings of the period are included but others are not; some statutorily listed modern buildings are included but others are not; and some untried and even unbuilt examples are included while some very prominent and well known modern buildings are not. Ultimately, this is a representative selection of modern buildings in Ulster rather than a definitive one.

A purist strain of Modernism may be detected in many of the buildings selected - in terms of abstract expression, mechanistic quality, and minimalist conception - but in others such simplicity of vision may be compromised and the repertoire of forms more all-inclusive. The authors acknowledge that the architectural expression and formal vocabulary is not entirely consistent throughout the selection and so perhaps the only constantly applied criterion is that each building in its own way adds something more to our understanding of what 'Modern' might mean at any one time.

The choice of geographical limits derives from the UAHS's long-standing recognition of the old province of Ulster as still forming a distinct region. It comprises the six counties of Northern Ireland – Antrim, Armagh, Down, Fermanagh, Londonderry, and Tyrone – and three 'border counties' in the Republic of Ireland – Cavan, Donegal, and Monaghan.

Although for much of the really formative period of modern architecture in Ireland from the 1920s to the 1940s, the creation of two separate states in 1921 and the clear political separation that was thereby effected meant that the southern counties of Cavan, Donegal and Monaghan related to a different set of architectural personalities and building preoccupations from those pertaining in Northern Ireland, they had previously, prior to 1920, been an integral part of the one entity. Later, by the 1950s despite continued political separation, one of those border counties, Donegal, became part of the Northern Irish architectural scene again, by dint of the leading Irish church architect Liam McCormick having his office in Northern Ireland but his home in the Republic where he was also to build his most significant works.

More recently, the increasingly international and cosmopolitan tendency in architecture worldwide, which has led to international and state boundaries being transcended by itinerant or migrant architects, has seen the architectural worlds of Northern Ireland and the Republic drawn into a closer conjunction than at any time since the Edwardian era. Thus, there may be renewed grounds for consideration of the old nine counties of Ulster as an architectural entity in itself.

[1]
Colquhoun, A. *Modern architecture*. Oxford: Oxford University Press, 2002. 9.

PAUL LARMOUR

St Conal's Church

PART ONE

ESSAY ONE PAUL LARMOUR

Modern Movement Architecture in Ulster 1900 to 1950

PAUL LARMOUR

The 20th century was one of rapidly changing ideas, fashions and tastes which saw a great diversity of architectural style in Western architecture, but through it all, one movement – the Modern Movement – stood out as encapsulating the essential spirit and energy of the times.

In international terms the seeds of the Modern Movement were sown at the start of the century with the development of new structural techniques, namely reinforced concrete and skeletal steel framing, and the subsequent and gradual departure from historical revivalism. The most important pioneering work was carried out on the continent of Europe which led to the formulation of Modernist theories and practices in such countries as Germany, France and Holland by the early 1920s. The approaches to Modernism varied greatly but ultimately a common language and expression were established and an almost universal idiom adopted.

Despite some of the pioneers' avowed aversion to 'stylism', the much-espoused 'functionalist' approach, shared by many across Europe, had evolved into a distinct style in itself for which the term 'International Style' was eventually coined. It was mainly characterized by white walls of plain concrete or smooth render, flat roofs, large horizontal windows, and a general avoidance of ornamentation. In the fullness of time this restricted palette was to be enhanced by the addition of other materials to the repertoire, such as brickwork and natural stone, and a greater variety of expression eventually became apparent.

The effects of this revolution in architectural design and aesthetics can be seen in Ulster from the late 1920s onwards as the work of the international pioneers and their followers became known, but it was a slow and tentative process.[1] In Ulster, as was largely the case in the rest of Ireland, native conservatism meant that architecture remained tied to tradition for much of the first half of the 20th century, irrespective of avant garde developments elsewhere. Northern Ireland in particular was not a very

1.0
Royal Victoria Hospital,
Belfast (1900-3),
by Henman and Cooper.
End elevation of ward block
with ventilation turrets.
ROYAL VICTORIA HOSPITAL

1.1
Interior: Albion factory,
Belfast (1908-9),
by Watt and Tulloch.
ARCHIVAL PHOTOGRAPH

1.2
Roof garden, Mater Hospital
Belfast (1900),
by William Fennell.
IRISH BUILDER, 1902

1.3
Women's Hostel,
Station Island, Lough Derg,
Co Donegal (1910-2),
by W.A.Scott.
ARCHIVAL PHOTOGRAPH

1.4
Grandstand with
refreshment rooms under,
Balmoral showgrounds,
Belfast (1920),
by T.W. Henry.
FERRO-CONCRETE, APRIL 1930

1.1

1.2

1.3

1.4

ripe field for architectural revolution: political and cultural attachment to England and the rest of the United Kingdom meant that traditional British values in architecture, as manifested in historic style revivals, were paramount here.

When the new state of Northern Ireland was founded in 1921 and formally separated from the rest of Ireland (which was initially called the Irish Free State, but from 1949 became known as the Republic of Ireland) the neo-Georgian style was favoured for the government's new building campaign. This covered police stations, telephone exchanges, post offices, employment exchanges, and some schools and technical colleges, with the main monuments of the new state - such as Parliament Buildings and the Royal Courts of Justice in Belfast - being wrought in a full-blooded neo-Classical manner. Most new banks in the inter-war era were also in some form of Classical or neo-Georgian style following on from the tradition of the Edwardian era, while most private houses of an architectural nature perpetuated the traditional forms of the English domestic revival of the late Victorian to Edwardian era. Traditional values were so dominant in the inter-war era that church architecture in its entirety in Northern Ireland, and indeed in the three southern Irish border counties of Ulster, conformed to a historic revivalist manner, whether of Gothic, Romanesque or Classical type.

It was against such a conservative and well entrenched traditional architectural background in Ulster in the inter-war era[2] that some occasional and isolated excursions into overt Modernism were made in the late 1920s. Some of the seeds of change had been evident much earlier, although centred largely on constructional or technological arrangements rather than any conscious striving for a new form of architectural expression.

Right at the very outset of the 20th century Belfast had witnessed an unexpected technological revolution in architecture, in the case of the Royal Victoria Hospital of

1.5
1.6

1900-3 (now demolished). With its particular arrangement of the Plenum system of forced ventilation, it can lay claim to being the first major building in the world to have been fully air-conditioned for human comfort. Designed by Henman and Cooper of Birmingham, its stylistic treatment was, however, entirely conventional being an adaptation of English Renaissance.[3] At the same time, another Belfast hospital, the Mater Infirmorum, a fairly dull Tudoresque red brick building opened in 1900 to the designs of William Fennell, had its ward blocks built with flat roofs covered with Vulcanite, a hard bituminous material, on top of which were then laid pathways and beds of grass, an early forerunner of the roof-terrace or 'gardens in the sky' concept which was to preoccupy some continental Modernists in the 1920s.

Shortly afterwards some of the earliest essays in reinforced concrete design in Ireland were built in Belfast to the designs of local architects using the French-originated Hennebique system. These included Somerset's linen warehouse[4] of 1904-5 by W.J.W. Roome, and the Albion factory in Wellwood Street of 1908-9 (now demolished) by Watt and Tulloch, but although the structural approach was new their external appearance, in red brick with slated roofs, was not. Another early example in Belfast of this pioneering system, the Monarch Laundry of 1907, on Donegall Road, designed by Jackson Smyth, was only inadvertently more 'modern' looking; its flat roof, which was used for the drying of laundry, being originally intended mainly for ease of adding a second storey, which was not built. In any case, its exterior walls of rock-faced concrete blocks gave an illusion of traditional masonry construction.

Meanwhile, at Station Island in Lough Derg, Co Donegal, one of the main pilgrimage sites in Ireland, the southern Irish-based Arts and Crafts architect William Scott of Dublin built the flat-roofed Women's Hostel of 1910-12 (now demolished) entirely of reinforced concrete, an unusual experiment but one which did not develop into any more fully developed interest in the more elemental or abstract qualities of architecture at that time.[5]

1.7   1.8

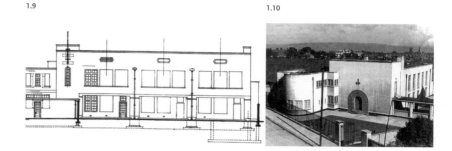

1.9   1.10

1.5
Grain silos, Avoniel Distillery,
Belfast (1920),
by Tulloch and Fitzsimons.
FERRO-CONCRETE, APRIL 1930

1.6
Design: St Patrick's School,
Belfast,
by R.S. Wilshere.
ARCHITECT AND BUILDING NEWS, 1928

1.7
Bank of Ireland,
Royal Ave, Belfast (1928-30)
by Joseph Downes of
McDonnell and Dixon
of Dublin.
PAUL LARMOUR 1980

1.8
Design: Linfield School
(now called Blythefield),
Belfast (1929-31),
by R.S. Wilshere.
ARCHITECTS' JOURNAL, 1931

1.9
Drawing:
Porter's Memorial School,
Belfast (1931),
by R.S. Wilshere.

1.10
Finiston School extension,
Belfast (1931-4),
by R.S. Wilshere.
PHOTOGRAPH BY ARCHITECT

It was a decade later before any Ulster-based architects produced a really frank expression of reinforced concrete construction, as demonstrated in such Hennebique structures as the grandstand and refreshment rooms at Balmoral agricultural showgrounds in Belfast, designed by Thomas Henry in 1920, and the grandstand at Ravenhill rugby ground in Belfast, designed by Hobart and Heron in 1923, but like the numerous Hennebique-system bridges of the period in Ulster, these buildings belong more to the field of engineering, and did not in themselves lead to a new direction in Ulster architecture. The same may be said of both the Sale Room at Balmoral showgrounds designed for the Royal Ulster Agricultural Society again by Thomas Henry in 1920 (now demolished), and the grain silos at Avoniel Distillery in Belfast designed by Tulloch and Fitzsimons in 1920 (now demolished), both with elevations of rectilinear design, built of reinforced concrete, displaying a complete absence of ornamentation, and both clearly architectural works, but presumably too plain to inspire any following.

It was not until the late 1920s that the first significant attempts at overtly modern design in the more established realm of architecture appeared in Northern Ireland. In 1928 an unbuilt design for St Patrick's Public Elementary School in Belfast by the city's schools' architect Reginald Wilshere, recently arrived from England, was considered sufficiently modern in spirit for the perspective drawing of it to have been used by the English journal *The Architect and Building News* as the headpiece to its article 'Modernism in architecture'.[6] That same year, 1928, the young Dublin architect Joseph Downes, working for the Dublin firm of McDonnell and Dixon, designed the Bank of Ireland in Royal Avenue, Belfast, in a similarly rectilinear idiom expressive of its steel-framed structure, but made less severe by the addition of a corner cupola and also enriched by Art Deco details. Completed in 1930 it was widely credited with introducing the modern style to Belfast.[7]

Also dating from the end of the 1920s was Linfield (now called Blythefield) School in Belfast (1929-31), designed by Reginald Wilshere. Flat-roofed and built of red brick

1.11   1.12   1.13   1.14

with each of its windows enclosed in a complete reinforced concrete surround in order to minimize any unequal loading due to the subsoil conditions, it was described at the time as 'a perfect example of modern work, the design being dictated by the construction'.[8] It was followed immediately afterwards by Wilshere's flat-roofed and rendered extensions to both Porter's Memorial School, designed in 1931, where the flat roof provided a playground on what was at the time a very congested site, and Finiston School (1931-4; now demolished), which, in addition to its curved bay and corner window, also showed the influence of the Dutch Modernist Willem Dudok in its entrance doorway.

Meanwhile, in the early 1930s, the Bank of Ireland followed up its pioneering work of Modernism in Belfast with another thoroughly modern building in Larne, Co Antrim (1932-3) and a further, less striking, example at Bangor, Co Down (1934), both designed by A.G.C. Millar of Dublin.

It was also architects from outside the province who provided the design for the most notable modern building of the inter-war period in Ulster, the King's Hall, a large exhibition hall built for the Royal Ulster Agricultural Society at Balmoral showgrounds, Belfast, in 1933-4 (now remodelled). It was designed by Archibald Leitch and Partners of London. A powerful piece of engineer's architecture, it comprised a glazed skeleton of reinforced concrete arches and stiffening panels, constructed using the Considère system, with vertical lantern lights running the whole length of the stepped roof. A few Art Deco details are its only concession to ornamentation.

Local architects exclusively, however, were involved in the domestic field in the 1930s in the design of Modernist villas, which had been one of the foremost vehicles for modern architectural design on the continent since the early 1920s. By 1925 the building type had reached Britain, introduced by the German architect Peter Behrens in a house at Northampton, and by the early 1930s it had arrived in Northern Ireland,

1.11
Bank of Ireland,
Larne, Co Antrim (1932-3),
by A.G.C. Millar of Dublin.
PAUL LARMOUR 1980

1.12 – 1.13
The King's Hall,
Belfast (1933-4),
by A. Leitch and Partners
of London.
ARCHIVAL PHOTOGRAPHS

1.14
House at Lismoyne Park,
Belfast (1932),
by Young and Mackenzie.
PAUL LARMOUR 1982

1.15
House at Antrim Road,
Belfast (1934),
by Hugh Gault.
PAUL LARMOUR 1982

1.16
Thesis design model for
Social and Sports Club
on Lough Neagh (1932),
by Philip Bell.

1.17
House at King's Road,
Belfast (1934),
by Philip Bell.
GP & RH BELL

1.18
'House on a hill': sketch
design for a house at
Killinchy, Co Down (1935),
by Philip Bell.

1.15 1.16 1.17 1.18

appearing first at Lismoyne Park in Belfast in a house designed by the local firm of Young and Mackenzie in 1932 for the builders D. McCune and Son.⁹ Of two storeys with a sun room on top of the flat roof, the house was built of white-painted rendered walls with stepped parapets and parapet railings to the roof, and horizontally arranged glazing bars to the metal window frames. It was followed in 1933 by two houses in Belfast with similar characteristics, designed by Hugh Gault – his own house at Lismoyne Park and one at Cooldarragh Park. Gault went on to design two more such houses in Belfast, at Antrim Road in 1934 and Cleaver Gardens in 1937.

Another Belfast architect, T. Dalton Purdy, was responsible for designing another local modern house which was to receive special publicity. That was the house built to his design in 1934 at Beverley Hills in Bangor, Co Down, for the builder and owner R.J. Shannon, which was featured in articles in both the local press and the *Irish Builder*, an architectural journal published in Dublin.¹⁰

Other examples of such flat-roofed modern houses, the most typical modern building type of the 1930s in British and Irish architecture, of which over forty were built in Ulster,¹¹ include no 5 Waterloo Park, Belfast, designed by Robert Sharp Hill in 1934; two designed by Anthony Lucy, at 9A Ascot Gardens, Belfast in 1935, and at Belmont Drive, Belfast in 1937; and a number designed by Philip Bell, the most committed Modernist of this period in Ulster.

Philip Bell from Lurgan in Co Armagh was one of the first university-trained architects in Ireland, having studied at the Liverpool School of Architecture from 1927 to 1932 where he became aware of contemporary developments in modern architecture internationally. His final-year thesis design of 1932, a proposal for a social and sports club on Lough Neagh in Northern Ireland, displayed all the hallmarks of the emergent International Style, with its bold projecting curved bay, flat roofs, sun terraces, corner windows and porthole windows. Returning to Ulster to set up his own practice in

1.19   1.20   1.21

Lurgan in 1933 he deployed these characteristic features on a number of buildings mostly in domestic architecture.

In 1934 Bell designed a flat-roofed house of fragmented cubic form, with a porthole window - one of the first instances in Ulster of this typical Modernist feature - at King's Road, Belfast (since remodelled). It was followed in 1935 by a house at Ballydorn Road, Killinchy, Co Down. Described as a 'House on a hill' on a preliminary sketch, the building is spread over a hilltop in two storeys, taking advantage of the views and the sunshine, with a south facing curved bay which suggests the influence of Wells Coates' highly publicised 'Sunspan' show-house exhibited at Olympia in London the previous year. Inside, a more free approach to planning than usual in Modernist houses in Ulster is apparent with the living room and dining room separated only by a change in level. Hitherto the conventionally compartmented arrangement of such houses in Ulster had failed to match the modernity of the exterior styling.

Well-known for his passion for boats, Bell inevitably attracted a number of commissions from the sailing fraternity. In 1935 he designed a small clubhouse at Whiterock, Co Down, for the Snipe Sailing Club. It was a simple single-storey timber-boarded building treated in a modern manner, flat-roofed with such nautical features as external stairs and parapet railings. It had a short life, however, as it was destroyed by fire and was replaced in 1936 by a larger building designed by Bell for what became known as the Strangford Lough Yacht Club. Reminiscent of his thesis design in some respects, the new clubhouse (now demolished) was an accomplished exercise in the International Style, nicely adapted to its site with its white rendered cubic and curved forms raised above a rusticated concrete plinth which projected out into the rock-strewn shore.

Contemporary with these clubhouses at Whiterock was Bell's commission around 1935-6 to design a group of four white rendered flat-roofed houses on the other side of the road,

1.22

1.23   1.24

1.25

as holiday homes for sailing enthusiasts, followed in 1937 by a small single-storey tea-shop (later remodelled), flat-roofed with a porthole window, to cater for visitors to the bay.

Elsewhere in the 1930s Bell designed a two-storey Modernist house of cubic form and compact plan at Moyallen, Co Down (1936), and a single-storey house of more expansive type, again flat-roofed with a broad curved window to the main living area, at Kircubbin, Co Down (1938).

Another committed Modernist in the 1930s was John McBride Neill of Belfast whose remodelling of the Savoy Hotel in Bangor, Co Down in 1933 was one of the earliest and most streamlined examples of the International Style in Ulster, of bold simplicity with rounded corners and banded glazing. As a specialist designer of cinemas, Neill was responsible for some of the most characteristic examples in Ulster, working in an overtly Modernist manner that moved from Art Deco façades with futuristic details to the more muted language of the International Style.[12]

Neill's pre-war cinemas in Belfast include the Apollo, Ormeau Road (1933; now remodelled) whose step-form Art Deco front in white roughcast initiated a new stylistic treatment for cinemas in Ulster; the remodelling of the Picturedrome, Mountpottinger Road (1934; now demolished) also in Art Deco style; the Majestic, Lisburn Road (1935-6; now remodelled) with tall corner windows to the stair towers and unusual rounded ends to the horizontal windows between them; the Troxy, Shore Road (1935-6; now demolished) and the Curzon, Ormeau Road (1935-6; now demolished), both of which featured an illuminated glass tower on the front; and the Forum, Crumlin Road (1937; now demolished) whose front façade was dominated by two vertical fins which curved back over the parapet giving the building a futuristic appearance.

Elsewhere in Ulster in the pre-war period Neill designed the Tonic, Bangor, Co Down (1935; now demolished), in its time the largest cinema in Northern Ireland and the

1.26   1.27   1.28

second largest in the whole of Ireland;[13] the Regal, Larne, Co Antrim (1935-7; now remodelled); and one at Omagh, Co Tyrone (1938; now demolished), the crisp functionalist façade of which was dominated by a broad expanse of metal windows bisected by a metal-framed glass tower, while the interior featured a series of porthole-like recessed lights.

Neill was particularly successful at carrying the modernistic treatment of his exteriors through to the interiors where his work was particularly marked by smooth lines and subtle curves, with skilful use of concealed lighting, reflecting the best continental examples of the time. As the press noted of one of his cinema interiors, the Strand of 1935, 'functionalism is ... the dominant idea. Everything is streamlined and horizontal, and every corner is rounded.'[14]

Neill was the leading cinema specialist in Ulster and his mature work can claim to rank with the best anywhere else in the British Isles in the heyday of the 1930s, but his works were not alone in that field. Other noteworthy cinemas of the period in Belfast[15] included the Broadway, Falls Road (1936; now demolished) by Thomas McLean, the Stadium, Shankill Road (1935-7; now demolished) by Robert Sharp Hill, and the Ambassador, Cregagh Road (1936; now remodelled) by John McGeagh, while the Vogue, Kilkeel, Co Down (1938) by Ben Cowser[16] is the only one to survive completely intact.

The Modernist traits in Reginald Wilshere's early Belfast schools had been overshadowed by a greater attachment to historical styling, most of his work in the 1920s being in neo-Georgian or collegiate Tudor mode, but from the early 1930s onwards his approach was to be predominantly modern. Traditional values were still apparent in his choice of materials and range of forms, with walls of rustic brickwork and some pitched roofs covered with red Roman tiles, but the stylistic idiom was to change, with strong hints of contemporary German, Scandinavian, and Dutch design

1.26
Interior: Curzon Cinema,
Belfast (1935-6),
by J.McB. Neill.
ARCHIVAL PHOTOGRAPH 1980s

1.27
Tonic Cinema,
Bangor, Co Down (1935),
by J.McB. Neill.
MAUREEN JOHNSTON COLLECTION

1.28
Drawing: Interior of the
Tonic Cinema,
Bangor, Co Down (1935),
by J.McB. Neill.
JOHN T DAVIS COLLECTION

1.29
Drawing: Cinema at Omagh,
Co Tyrone,
by J,McB. Neill.
JOHN T DAVIS COLLECTION

1.30
Interior: Stadium Cinema,
Belfast (1935-7),
by Robert Sharp Hill.
Contemporary photograph.
HOGG COLLECTION, ULSTER MUSEUM

1.31
Drawing: Ambassador Cinema,
Belfast (1936),
by John MacGeagh

1.32
Vogue Cinema,
Kilkeel, Co Down (1938),
by Ben Cowser.
PAUL LARMOUR 1990

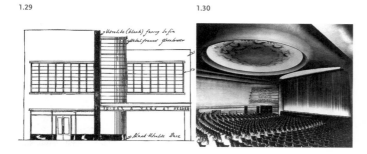

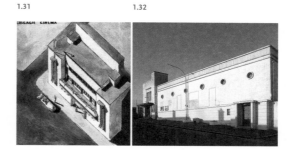

apparent, characterized by the use of flat roofs, large areas of glazing and windows arranged in horizontal bands as well as featuring 'corner' and 'porthole' types.

Typical examples of such schools were Avoniel (1933-5), Argyle (1933-7; now demolished), Nettlefield (1934-6), Edenbrooke (1934-7), Cliftonville (1936-8), Beechfield (1937-8), Grove (1937-9), and Charters' Memorial (1939-51; now demolished). Particularly notable are Botanic School of 1936-9 where the steep fall of the sloping site was used to form an 'amphitheatre' in the courtyard for such functions as outdoor teaching and an open-air theatre;[17] and McQuiston Memorial School (now called the School of Music) of 1934-6, a three-storey cubic block with a roof-top playground which was necessitated by the lack of space on the ground. McQuiston Memorial School was acknowledged in the press at the time as 'Belfast's most advanced example of the 'new' architecture'.[18]

Aside from their up-to-date styling, much of it influenced by Willem Dudok, Wilshere's schools were revolutionary here for their planning, being provided with separate rooms for each class, special facilities for certain subjects, efficient ventilation, open-air corridors, and carefully considered lighting. Indeed these were not only the first really 'modern' schools to be built anywhere in Ireland but were considered to be among the best in the British Isles. They were not only regularly featured in the English architectural press, Wilshere being publicized there more than any other Irish architect of the period, but examples of his work were also included in the exhibition of international schools' architecture organized by the Royal Institute of British Architects in 1938, and in Wright and Gardner-Medwin's book *The Design of Nursery and Elementary Schools* published in 1938,[19] which was also international in scope.

In addition to his schools Wilshere also designed some associated buildings in a similar vein, such as the caretaker's house at Carr's Glen School (1938-40), flat-roofed with a

1.33

1.34

1.35

shallow bowed front, and an equally stylish combined pavilion and groundsman's house (1935-6; now remodelled) at Ormeau Playing Fields in Belfast.

Of inter-war schools elsewhere in Ulster, only The Model in Londonderry of 1937 designed by J.H. Brown approached those of Wilshere in Belfast for modern styling albeit more severely treated.

Although Wilshere, Bell and Neill were the most committed to modern design of Northern Ireland's architects in the 1930s there were some notable works designed by others. The modernistic Telephone House of 1932-5 in Belfast, designed by the chief government architect Roland Ingleby Smith and his assistant Thomas Rippingham, which was steel-framed with Art Deco motifs to vertically recessed window panels, was one rare departure from its architects' usual neo-Georgian manner; another was the more horizontally stressed GPO Sorting Office at Smithfield in Belfast, designed in 1938 by Rippingham alone, but now demolished. The Art Deco fronted Sinclair's Store of 1935 in Royal Avenue, Belfast, designed by James Scott, was a conspicuous local response to the pioneering Bank of Ireland of 1928-30 opposite. David Boyd produced one of the best known examples of the International Style in Ulster, at the Floral Hall in Bellevue recreational grounds (now the zoo), Antrim Road, Belfast (1935-6), a popular concert and dance hall with cafés, built of smooth white walls with a large shallow domed rotunda. Meanwhile at Lisnagarvey Radio Transmitting Station, Co Down, of 1935-6, the London architects Wimperis, Simpson and Guthrie continued to underline the credentials of the modern style for buildings of more indisputably modern function. A building of comparable type was the electricity sub-station at Glen Road, Braniel, Belfast, flat-roofed and smooth-rendered with a bowed elevation, dating from the 1930s but of unknown authorship.

Elsewhere in Ulster, beyond Northern Ireland, the most notable development in a modern style was the building of alcohol factories at Carndonagh, Labbadish and

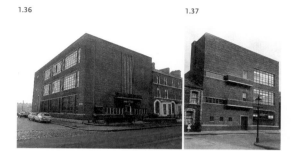

1.36   1.37   1.38

Convoy in Co Donegal between 1935 and 1938, part of a series commissioned by the southern Irish government. Of unusual construction, comprising steel framing with bolted steel cladding, they were designed by the Dutch architect J.D. Postma in a severely functionalist manner that suited their industrial character.

Despite the growing interest in the modern style and its demonstrably wide range of applications, one building type that was unaffected was churches. In a field that was completely dominated by historical styles, the Belfast architect Denis O'D Hanna's speculative unbuilt 'design for a modern church' published in 1934 was the nearest that anyone came to breaching the last bastion of traditional revivalism in Ulster architecture between the wars.

Due to the Second World War, in which Northern Ireland, as part of the United Kingdom, was directly involved, there was very little building work during the early 1940s. A similar situation prevailed in the south of Ireland, where, although the Irish Free State had adopted a neutral position during the war, building was still curtailed by a shortage of building materials. It was not until the immediate post-war period that normal building activity was to be resumed and there were to be any significant additions to the stock of modern architecture in Ulster.

There were a few buildings put up during the war years in Northern Ireland mainly by the government, and some of them connected with the war effort. One of the most interesting but least conspicuous was the control tower at Langford Lodge airfield near Crumlin, Co Antrim, built in 1942. Very plain and utilitarian, with flat roofs and rendered walls it had its windows set in an angled plane canted out at the top for greater clarity of vision in all conditions, an unusual detail for the time. As military airfield control towers were normally designed and built by the Air Ministry, this one appears to be unique in the whole of the United Kingdom in that it was designed and built by the Ministry of Aircraft Production.

Meanwhile the architectural staff of the Northern Ireland Office of Works were involved in some housing schemes, all in a modern idiom, built of rustic brick with concrete surrounds to openings, mono-pitch roofs, and some porthole windows. These include a small group of semi-detached houses for power-station workers at Ballylumford, Co Antrim, dating from 1943, a similar group for the Ministry of Supply at Laurelvale, Co Armagh, dating from 1944, and a much larger estate of mainly terraced houses for the Admiralty at Antrim town, also dating from 1944, all designed by Thomas Rippingham. Rippingham also designed the physical education centre, called the Henry Garrett Building, at Stranmillis College, the state-funded teachers' training college in Belfast, in 1944. Whereas pre-war work on the Stranmillis campus had been of a traditional type this building marked the change to a more modern idiom.

Beyond the realm of government building in the early 1940s, there was a group of flat-roofed white-rendered semi-detached houses at Larne, Co Antrim, designed by James Scott in 1944, and an extensive canteen for Gallaher's tobacco factory at North Queen Street, Belfast, designed in 1943 by Samuel Stevenson and Sons in a modern style with segmental vaulted concrete roofs. A similar structural arrangement was used again in 1946 for Gallaher's sample rooms at Severn Street, Belfast, this time by Gallaher's Architectural Department. Also in the early 1940s there was a pair of what were termed 'experimental' semi-detached flat-roofed houses built at Ballynafeigh, Belfast, designed in 1943 by Denis O'D Hanna with brick walls but otherwise consisting of prefabricated reinforced concrete construction; they proved slow to sell due to concerns that so much concrete would make them cold to live in.

With the end of the war in 1945 new building grew apace. The first big project was the building of Cregagh housing estate in Belfast in 1945-9, designed by Thomas Rippingham of the Ministry of Finance on behalf of the newly formed Northern Ireland Housing Trust. The scarcity of some materials at the time determined the

1.43 1.44

1.45 1.46

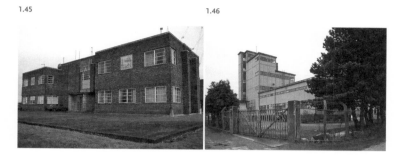

strictly utilitarian type of design and structure, characterized by the use of flat concrete roofs. The estate was notable for having continuous frontages, with no unsightly views of back gardens, and a varied layout of terraces, closes, and small squares. The central open space was occupied by Cregagh Primary School, built in 1949 for Down Education Committee (but now demolished), also to a design by Rippingham which consisted of staggered cubic blocks in rustic brick with corner glazing and porthole windows.

Cregagh Estate was the most admired housing development of its time in Northern Ireland, drawing visiting delegations of architects and housing officials from Britain during the 1940s to study its layout, and subsequently winning the Housing Medal awarded by the Ministry of Health in 1951 for the best post-war estate in Northern Ireland, but despite its success there were very few other housing schemes in the same architectural idiom here, the majority of them perpetuating the traditional pitched-roofed house-type. Exceptions were the white-walled flat-roofed Whitewell Estate of 1947 in Belfast, designed by the Housing Trust's own architects; some flat-roofed houses at the Mount Vernon Estate in Belfast designed by R.S. Wilshere in 1948; some flat-roofed flats and shops of 1947 at Merville Garden Village, Whitehouse, and flats, shops and houses of 1949 at Abbot's Cross Garden Village, Whiteabbey, both near Belfast, all designed by E. Prentice Mawson of London; and an estate of mono-pitch-roofed houses at Lisburn, Co Antrim, by the firm of Philip Bell and his brother Roger.

Philip Bell's pre-war commitment to the Modern Movement was undiminished in the immediate post-war period. At the single-storey McCullough House of 1945 in Glenavy he continued the International Style manner of white walls, flat roof, corner window, and continuous glazing to a curved bay. Some of these features reappeared in his proposal for a prototype modern farmhouse prepared for the Ministry of Agriculture in the 1940s but never built, and also in his unusual double-house of 1946

1.47

1.48   1.49

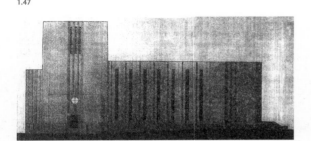

at Lisanally Lane, Armagh for a pair of private clients, comprising a two-storey house joined to a single-storey bungalow, characterized by blocky cubic forms and featuring floor-to-ceiling glazing and glass brick screens.

Nearby, and dating from the same year, 1946, Bell was also responsible for the Alexander Crescent housing development in Armagh, a 60-unit estate of flat-roofed terrace and semi-detached dwellings designed for the local council. Like other Modernist housing schemes of the time, however, the units were of a traditional compartmented plan-type and were merely styled in the manner of the 'new architecture'.

Reginald Wilshere, the prolific Belfast Education Architect, also carried on his well-established pre-war modern manner into the 1940s, as at Wheatfield Primary School an impressively large three-storey building with flat roofs and many porthole windows, designed in 1949 in his favoured rustic brick. Elsewhere, however, he extended his repertoire to include prefabricated aluminium units for such largely single-storey schools as Annadale Grammar School, Annadale Avenue, designed in 1948 (now demolished), and Ashfield Girls' High School, Holywood Road, and Sydenham Primary School, Strandburn Street, both designed in 1949. The units were manufactured by Short Brothers and Harland Ltd of Belfast using what was called the 'Bristol' system, which had originally been devised by the Bristol Aeroplane Company of Weston-Super-Mare. This development represented Ulster architecture's first concentrated excursion into prefabrication and system building, something which had occupied the minds of Modern Movement architects elsewhere for many years. It was a system adopted out of necessity here, owing to the shortage of traditional building materials, but was also attractive due to the speed with which buildings could be erected. Sydenham Primary School, which was in use by 1950 and was the first new school in Belfast since the war, had its aluminium wings – the major part of the building – erected in only 75 days.

1.47
Design for a modern church,
by Denis O'D. Hanna.
IRISH BUILDER, 1934

1.48
Airfield control building,
Langford Lodge,
Co Antrim (1942),
by the Ministry of Aircraft
Production.
PAUL LARMOUR 1999

1.49
Housing at Laurelvale,
Co Armagh (1944),
by Thomas Rippingham.
PAUL LARMOUR 1993

1.50
Cregagh Housing Estate,
Belfast (1945–9),
by Thomas Rippingham.
W.D. FRY

1.51
Design for a modern
farmhouse for the Ministry
of Agriculture (1940s),
by Philip Bell.

1.52
Pair of houses at Lisanally
Lane, Armagh (1946),
by Philip Bell.
PAUL LARMOUR 1991

1.53
Wheatfield School,
Belfast (1949-52),
by R.S. Wilshere.
PHOTOGRAPH BY ARCHITECT

Along with housing and schools the main preoccupation throughout Northern Ireland in the immediate post-war era was the building of new factories, a type which was to spread the modern style of architecture to every sizeable town in the country. Among the more notable examples was the Down Shoes factory of 1947-9 at Banbridge, Co Down, designed by W.D.R. and R.T. Taggart, an impressive essay in International Style in brickwork with long sweeping lines, broad expanses of glazing including a continuously glazed single-storey curved bay, and with a free-standing curved porter's lodge to match. Others were the Taylor-Woods hosiery factory of 1948 at Enniskillen, Co Fermanagh, designed by the architects to the Ministry of Finance, with a similarly banded two-storey bay; Courtauld's vast rayon factory at Carrickfergus of 1948-50 designed by the company's architects in collaboration with the engineers Alexander Gibb and Partners; and the Bairnswear factory of 1950 at Armagh by Thomas Rippingham, an assured design with an impressive and elegant curved stairwell in the manner of the great German architect Erich Mendelsohn.

Private house building, such a popular vehicle of modern architecture before the war, was severely curtailed after it. Among the few examples in the 1940s to show any variation on the predominantly cubic box-like format of the 1930s was no 110 Malone Road, Belfast, a two-storey house built on a split level with a garage underneath part of the house and a mono-pitch roof overall, designed in 1949 by Henry Lynch-Robinson, an emerging young architect in Belfast who had trained at the Liverpool School of Architecture. Another was the Lynn house at Creevagh near Londonderry, a single-storey house with a flat concrete roof over walls of roughcast and natural stone, designed in 1948 by Liam McCormick of Londonderry, another young graduate of similar promise from the Liverpool school.[20] Much admired at the time (but now remodelled), the Lynn house achieved a certain amount of fame as the only Irish example to be included by F.R.S. Yorke in any of his numerous books surveying Modernist houses internationally.[21]

1.54   1.55   1.56

McCormick had been establishing his Modernist credentials with some minor jobs near where he lived in Co Donegal from the mid-1940s, including a flat-roofed mill office at Moville, and a reinforced concrete bathing shelter of 1947 also at Moville, before securing a commission for a sizeable school at Pennyburn, Londonderry (now demolished) which was designed in 1948 in conjunction with his partner Frank Corr. Thoroughly modern in style, of pre-cast concrete construction with flat concrete roofs and large areas of glazing, St Patrick's School was to show the influence of a visit McCormick had made with the Liverpool School of Architecture to see important modern buildings in Paris in 1937, in the use of random rubble stonework for the gables, inspired by Le Corbusier's Pavillon Suisse, and the use of pre-cast panels with exposed seashore pebbles, inspired by Beaudouin and Lods's school at Surêsnes.

More significantly for the future, however, 1948 saw McCormick and his partner gain first prize in the competition for the design of a new church at Ennistymon in Co Clare, in the Republic of Ireland. Their entry, influenced in style by contemporary Swiss church architecture, attracted a great deal of attention as an unexpectedly modern design in a field that had hitherto been dominated by designs of a traditional revivalist type, and launched the partnership, but McCormick in particular, on a long career at the forefront of modern church architecture throughout Ireland.

Henry Lynch-Robinson, meanwhile, was to underline his growing reputation in Belfast as a progressive young architect with his modernistic remodelling in 1950 of the Mayfair cinema façade in College Square East featuring an eye-catching array of bull's-eye vents and an aluminium fin, and being appointed that same year as 'Adviser on Design' to the Festival of Britain 1951 committee for Northern Ireland.

Just as the 20th century in Ulster had opened with an important hospital of revolutionary design by a visiting firm of architects so too did the first half of the century end. At Altnagelvin General Hospital in Londonderry, a former assistant of

1.54
Sydenham Primary School,
Belfast (1949-50),
by R.S. Wilshere.
PAUL LARMOUR 1991

1.55
Down Shoes factory,
Banbridge, Co Down (1947-9),
by W.D.R. and R.T. Taggart.
PAUL LARMOUR 1993

1.56
Bairnswear factory,
Armagh (1950),
by Thomas Rippingham.
PHOTOGRAPH BY ARCHITECT

1.57
House on Malone Road,
Belfast (1949),
by Henry Lynch-Robinson.
A & C PHOTOGRAPHY

1.58
House at Creevagh,
Londonderry (1948-9),
by W.H.D. McCormick.
PHOTOGRAPH BY ARCHITECT

1.59
St Patrick's School, Pennyburn,
Londonderry (1948-54),
by F. Corr and
W.H.D. McCormick.
PAUL LARMOUR 1992

1.60
Design: Altnagelvin Hospital,
Londonderry (1948-9),
by Yorke, Rosenberg and
Mardall, of London.
ARCHITECTURAL REVIEW, 1949

1.57 1.58

1.59 1.60

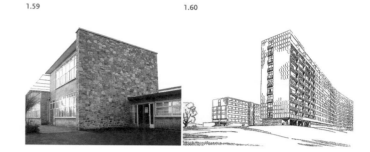

Le Corbusier in Paris, the Czech-born Eugene Rosenberg of the firm of Yorke Rosenberg and Mardall of London, in his initial designs of 1948-9 brought to Ulster the Corbusian idea of tall modern blocks set in an open landscape. It was not only the first entirely new hospital to be built after the start of the Health Service but also the first hospital design of this kind in the United Kingdom, and although its extent was soon to be greatly reduced with the original configuration of blocks altered to a less elegant arrangement, the initial impact of the first published designs remained: Ulster had been demonstrably drawn into the mainstream of post-war modern architecture. The slow process of introducing Ulster to the shapes and forms, materials and ideals of the Modern Movement was over and a new generation of local architects, together with some accomplished visitors, were poised to develop the vision further.[22]

Notes and References

1 Some aspects of pre-war Modernism in Ulster architecture have been discussed or illustrated in the following publications: Larmour, P. The inter-war years in Belfast. *Big A3* (The Magazine of the Department of Architecture, QUB, Belfast), 1973 Unpaginated. Evans, D. *An introduction to modern Ulster architecture.* Belfast: UAHS, 1977. Larmour, P. *Belfast: an illustrated architectural guide.* Belfast: Friar's Bush Press, 1987.

2 A range of examples of traditional revivalist inter-war architecture, including the most notable examples, is illustrated in Larmour, P. *Belfast: an illustrated architectural guide,* Belfast: Friar's Bush Press, 1987.

3 Larmour, P. A revolution in hospital design. *Perspective,* 4(3),1996. 38-40. Larmour, P. Royal Victoria Hospital. In Becker, A. Olley, J. and Wang, W. (eds.) *20th century architecture: Ireland.* Munich & New York: Prestel Verlag, 1997. 90-91.

4 Larmour, P. A pioneering reinforced concrete building in Belfast: Somerset's factory in Hardcastle Street. *Ulster Architect,* (10), 1984. 12-16.

5 Larmour, P. 'The drunken man of genius': William A. Scott (1871-1921). *Irish Architectural Review,* 3, 2001. 24-41.

6 Modernism in architecture. *The Architect and Building News,* 25 May 1928. 766.

7 *Irish Builder and Engineer,* 28 September, 1929. 869; 1 March, 1930. 184; and 26 April, 1930. 366. *Belfast Telegraph Guide to Belfast,* 1934. 49. *Belfast News-Letter,* 9 September, 1938.

8 *Irish Builder and Engineer,* 19 December, 1931. 1090.

9 A modern Belfast house. *Belfast News-Letter,* 8 April, 1933.

10 A modern home in Bangor. *Belfast News-Letter,* 13 December, 1934; A modern house. *Irish Builder and Engineer,* 3 November, 1934. 938. The exterior of the house has now been remodelled.

11 A number of them appear in a list provided by this author for the following publication:

Gould, J. Gazetteer of modern houses in the United Kingdom and the Republic of Ireland. *Twentieth Century Architecture,* 2, 1996. 126.

12 Larmour, P. The big feature (John McBride Neill 1905-1974). *Perspective,* 5(4),1997. 45-49.

13 Larmour, P. The Tonic Cinema. In Becker, A. Olley, J. and Wang, W. (eds.) *op cit.* 108-109.

14 *Belfast News-Letter,* 7 December, 1935. The interior of the building has now been remodelled and the exterior changed from the original.

15 Larmour, P. Cinema Paradiso (Cinema architecture of Belfast). *Perspective,* 4 (4),1996. 23-27.

16 Larmour, P. An architect of restrained modernism (Benjamin Cowser 1897-1981). *Perspective,* 3(5),1995. 43-45.

17 Larmour, P. Botanic Primary School. In Becker, A. Olley, J. and Wang, W. (eds.) *op cit.* 116.

18 *Belfast News-Letter,* 2 October, 1936.

19 Wright, H.M. and Gardner-Medwin, R. *The design of nursery and elementary schools.* London: Architectural Press, 1938. 58,92,108.

20 Larmour, P. In the name of the father (Liam McCormick 1916-1996). *Perspective,* 5 (2),1996. 30-43.

21 Yorke, F. and Whiting, P. *The new small house.* London: Architectural Press, 1953. 144.

22 Many of the buildings referred to here have already been demolished, or remodelled almost beyond recognition, during the last few decades, but a number of examples of Modern Movement architecture in Northern Ireland have been statutorily listed by the government, mainly as a result of two thematic surveys carried out by this author on behalf of the Environment and Heritage Service in the early 1990s, one on 'Post-1914 buildings' in general, and one on 'Post-Second World War buildings'.

PART ONE

ESSAY TWO DAVID EVANS

Modern Movement Architecture in Ulster 1950 to 2005

DAVID EVANS

2.0 – 2.1
Transport House, Belfast
(1956-9),
by J. J. Brennan.
E & M HIRSK 2006

Ulster is a small and somewhat isolated architectural community: self contained and introverted perhaps but, like a rock pool, it is continually refreshed by incoming tides and new arrivals. The population at close to one and a half million people is roughly equivalent to an average English county or a single large conurbation and is not large enough to sustain a major architectural culture. It has not yet produced a major Modernist architect but it can lay claim to a range of good Modernist design; there is, too, a growing awareness of context and the indigenous tradition in building. Provincial our architecture is, but perhaps it also touches on that 'parochialism' that the poet Patrick Kavanagh regarded as the basis of all great civilisations, it 'is universal' he wrote, 'it deals with fundamentals'.[1]

The geographical scope of this book, as discussed in the introduction, is the ancient province of Ulster. It bridges two different countries and two markedly different architectural cultures and the range of buildings included benefits from this diversity. If Northern Ireland tends towards introversion the Republic of Ireland is now seen as more outward looking and can also claim, in Michael Scott, a leading European Modernist as one of its own. One of Scott's partners, Robin Walker, had worked in the offices of Le Corbusier on the Marseilles Unité and later with Mies van der Rohe; another, Ronnie Tallon, transplanted Mies to Irish soil. Another Irish practitioner, Shane de Blacam, studied under Louis Kahn at Philadelphia – this kind of rich hinterland together with the continental experience gained in Paris, Barcelona and Berlin by the rising generation has given Irish architecture a new confidence and maturity.

In the last fifty years the arts have flourished in Ulster's vibrant but divided society. Painting, music and drama thrive and the Ulster poets are internationally acclaimed. Against the background of the Troubles, architecture has had its successes but it is an art form that depends upon settled times and economic growth to prosper – conditions that were sadly missing through much of the 70s and 80s. Recent omens are good and over the last ten years a series of notable buildings has confirmed an upturn in architectural fortunes. Modernism, too, has had its good and bad times in the last half century. It has experienced the highs of the Festival of Britain and the lows of Postmodernism; it has weathered the lean 50s and the years of civil unrest and has come to terms with contextualism and heritage. It has had many successes but it has also had its failures; the Corbusier inspired high-rise housing has proved disastrous in many instances and the insensitive office buildings in urban centres have won few admirers. In the name of progress, the disappearance of so many well loved buildings in the 60s to make way for bland modern structures led to a public outcry. Such was the concern arising from the demolition of a series of buildings in the Queen's University area of Belfast that the Ulster Architectural Heritage Society was formed in 1967 to lobby for effective legislation to protect the architectural heritage which was eventually secured in 1972. In 1971 Charles Brett, the Society's chairman, writing on 'The Duty of the Architect towards Ulster's Architectural Heritage' was in serio-comic vein quoting a text from Deuteronomy 'Cursed be he that removeth his neighbour's landmark' and went on (in his own words) 'but blessed is he that proppeth it up and repaireth it and treateth it with respect'.[2]

Twenty years earlier, in 1951, the English architect and critic, Lionel Brett Viscount Esher, wondered why 'intelligent laymen who appreciate modern painting and music don't for some reason like modern architecture'. One explanation he suggested, 'might be that whereas painters and composers have their work reviewed and criticised in language that is intelligible to outsiders, there is no regular criticism of Modern architecture'.[3] How much the picture has changed since then is open to speculation but some outline of how Modernism came about seems appropriate here.

The date that divides the old from the new according to Reyner Banham 'is tacitly allowed to be somewhere around 1900'.[4] He cites the School of Art in Glasgow, by Charles Rennie Mackintosh and designed on both sides of 1900, as representing the first steps of Modernism in these islands. It is delicately balanced between old and new; it borrows heavily from the past but the honesty in the use of materials is modern as is the handling and detail of the timber roof-trusses where there is a 'solicitude for the visual identity of each member that is a consistent theme of Modern Architecture'. On the other hand Nikolaus Pevsner's analysis in *The Sources of Modern Architecture and Design* traces the roots of Modernism to the first industrial revolution, to Abraham Darby's iron bridge at Coalbrookdale in Shropshire (1771-81), to the Menai Suspension Bridge (1818-26) by Thomas Telford and to the Crystal Palace (1851) by Thomas Paxton, a prefabricated structure which represented 'the first major escape from historical styles in architecture'.[5]

In the early years of the last century the artistic world in Europe was apparently a cauldron of theories and proclamations: Expressionism, Futurism, Constructivism, Cubism, Purism, Dadaism, Surrealism, Suprematism and de Stijl, for example, which all touched on architecture and proclaimed a vision for the future and a rejection of the burden of history. Their coming together as a coherent philosophical system must have appeared unlikely but the Bauhaus, founded in Weimar by Walter Gropius in 1919, forged a kind of unanimity. The absorption and fusing together of these 'isms' became what is now understood as Modern Architecture which contains in its make up, in Nikolaus Pevsner's portentous words of 1968, 'that what is most disastrous in the visual arts of the 20th century and what is most hopeful [which] was fully in existence by time the Age of the World Wars dawned'.[6] The Bauhaus was a meeting point for designers and architects from all over Europe and America and its propaganda machine disseminated a coherent and consistent design message throughout the world. The publication in New York of *International Style* in 1932 celebrated the architecture that had arrived in the early 1920s and in Henry Russell Hitchcock's words 'developed to classic expression by 1930 and from that time on found wider and wider acceptance throughout the world so much so that by mid-century the International Style could even come to seem to many a characteristically American style'.[7]

It was not until 1951 and the Festival of Britain that widely accessible and fully developed expression of the new architecture came to these islands and although Modernism was by then half a century old the opening of the South Bank Exhibition aroused a tremulous note of excitement among younger architects. The words of Esher almost bring a tear to the eye in the light of the disillusion of the following years – 'for the first time in the misty sunlight of that fine May morning it was possible to feel that we witness here the long awaited opening flower of Modern Architecture'.[8] As Harold Meek commented, the exhibition introduced millions of people to architecture of almost uniformly high quality.[9] In its planning it broke with the Beaux Arts tradition of such exhibitions and pioneered a new informal approach. The *Architectural Review* claimed that the designs belonged to 'a tradition of non-stylistic architecture derived from a straightforward fulfilment of function and from the logical use of materials – the Functional Tradition'.[10] It was also festive architecture that delighted in intricacy, sky pattern and the interrupted view; it juxtaposed glass and canvas screens with massive concrete and stone walling and it 'hovered by nature and purpose on the borderline of fantasy, resting as lightly as a mirage on the water' as Linda Brooks noted was reported in the *Observer* at the time.[11]

History has been severe on the exhibition, dismissing it as fussy, folksy and over decorative. It was indeed a false dawn but it brought Modernism into the public realm and launched a talented generation of architects.

Britain had to wait until the Millennium projects for another concentrated burst of iconic and cultural buildings. These buildings include the Eden Project, Cornwall; the Great Court of the British Museum, the Millennium Dome and Tate Modern, London; the Lowry Centre at Salford Quays and Imperial War Museum North, Manchester; and the Gateshead Bridge and Sage Centre, Newcastle. They represent the flowering of the kind of innovative and high-tech Modernism that was foreshadowed at the South Bank in 1951.

2.2  2.3

Ulster in 1951 was generally neo-Georgian in taste. Denis O'D Hanna commented 'there is much to be said for this style, and, had it not been for the demand for novelty in the age, it might have lingered very profitably for a generation or two'.[12] However, change was in the air and Northern Ireland launched its own celebration of the Festival of Britain, organized by the Council for the Encouragement of Music and the Arts (CEMA) which was the forerunner of the Arts Council of Northern Ireland. In the same year the Royal Society of Ulster Architects, which was celebrating its golden jubilee, hosted the annual conference of the RIBA. Its programme, which included an architectural exhibition, held out 'a prospect of much profit and pleasure' in the words of R.H. Gibson the president of the RSUA.[13]

The design team for the Exhibition of Architecture consisted of James Scott, Denis O'D Hanna and Philip Bell together with Max Clendinning, Ian Campbell and Raymond Leith who were student members of the RSUA. The exhibition was held in Fountain Street, Belfast inside a blitzed building which had been made watertight. The aims were to promote interest in good contemporary architecture, to change the public's perception of the architect, and to show a concern for the physical environment in the widest sense. Passers-by were 'intrigued by the glass door to the tiled entrance foyer and the glimpse of the garden beyond'.[14] After a brief historical section there followed an exhibition of drawings, photographs and models of modern buildings which it was felt might influence development in Ulster. The visitor entered a full scale living room with a long side-wall in strong blue paintwork which extended through full-height glazing into the garden beyond 'to create the illusion of room and garden as one unit'.[15] The furniture which featured the splayed and tapered legs so characteristic of the period was designed by Max Clendinning who was 'considered to have made the greatest design contribution to the Festival in Ulster'. These are the words of Robert McKinstry who, looking back at the exhibition twenty years after in 1971, wrote 'it celebrated the aims of the Modern Movement with a clarity of vision that was never to occur again'.[16]

2.2 – 2.3
Exhibition of Architecture
Belfast (1951),
by James Scott, Denis O'D.
Hanna, Philip Bell with
Max Clendinning, Ian
Campbell, Raymond Leith.
IAN CAMPBELL

2.4 – 2.6
Microbiology Centre,
Royal Victoria Hospital, Belfast
(1961-5),
by Casson, Condor & Partners.
MARK HACKETT 2005

2.4   2.5   2.6

The Official Farm and Factory Exhibition at Castlereagh, organised by CEMA, included the Farmhouse of Tomorrow, designed by Henry Lynch Robinson, whose controversial house on the Malone Road, Belfast had announced his arrival as a Modernist. The farmhouse was part of a farm complex which included grain stores, a tower silo and a Dutch barn. The farmhouse was connected to this group by a covered way and was raised on stilts with garaging and storage below, the long open-plan kitchen-dining-living room was glazed from floor to ceiling and sliding doors opened to a long balcony.

In the 50s the home truths of the Festival of Britain – the fulfilment of function and the logical use of materials – were applied in earnest. 'Obedience to programme' was the watchword and design was governed, perhaps, more by the application of principle rather than by appearance, or by ethics rather than by aesthetics. Any taint of neo-Georgian symmetry was out. Flat roofs were in and new schools of the period tended towards informality in layout and widely spaced, continuously glazed classrooms to provide good natural lighting and cross-ventilation.

Greenwood School, Upper Newtownards Road, Belfast by Henry Lynch Robinson and Robert McKinstry (1954) and J.V.T. Scott's Forthill School, Lisburn (1957) are instances. St Patrick's School, Antrim Road, Belfast by McLean and Forte (1952) was one of many in Ulster to use the Orlit system of pre-cast concrete construction. Prefabrication was seen as the solution to the housing problem and an answer to a massive school building programme. Housing at Cregagh, Belfast by Thomas Rippingham in 1952 for the Northern Ireland Housing Trust used flat concrete roofs and mellow brickwork and maintained the inherent quality of his pre-war work in a cautious Modern idiom.

There was little scope for the private architect in these lean years and one of the few opportunities was the design of the private house. In a series of single-storey houses Houston & Beaumont pioneered 'a severe and simple version of the traditional farm-house but modern in the handling of space'.[17]

2.7

2.8

The phase New Brutalism entered the language in the mid-50s, spread like wildfire and is often loosely applied; it is particularly associated with the leading English architects of that time, Alison and Peter Smithson, who called for a return to the kind of uncompromising rigour that characterized the work of Mies van der Rohe and Le Corbusier and a revival of fundamental functionalist principles. It was a marked reaction to the populism of the South Bank Exhibition and the so-called Contemporary Style, or as the *Architectural Review* termed it the 'New Humanism', and it was characterized by shallow pitched roofs, brick walls and squarish picture windows in timber frames. It was widely used in the New Towns built around London. This Welfare State architecture was taken up locally by the Northern Ireland Housing Trust (later the Northern Ireland Housing Executive) but with a greater emphasis on the use of rendered walling rather than brickwork.

The invocation of the example set by the great European masters led to their work being adopted as the mould of form for the architecture of the 60s and beyond. The influence of Le Corbusier permeates the decade; pilotis carrying rectangular superstructures and overhanging storeys with attenuated columns became familiar motifs. The white blank walls and small windows of the Pilgrimage Church Ronchamp, 1950-54, reappeared in church architecture and the occasional public house.
If modern architecture is not a style, but a movement of truths, as its apostles claim, its forms can seem to follow fashion almost as closely as function. An early arrival in Ulster of the Corbusian repertoire is Transport House, Belfast by J.J. Brennan of Dublin, 1956-9. It features pilotis and the curved wall to High Street bearing a tiled mural recalls the staircase tower of the Pavilion Suisse, Cité Universitaire Paris 1930-32. The extension to the Ulster Museum and the Ashby Institute wear their Corb on their sleeves, and Casson, Condor & Partners Microbiology Centre at the Royal Victoria Hospital, Belfast with its taut, stretched skin façade and jutting balconies and stair-cases is a fusion of the Purist phase of early Corbusier and the sculptured exposed concrete of his post-war work.

2.9

2.10

These buildings are the work of English architects. The local profession, it seems, revealed something of the Ulsterman's innate caution and tendency to understatement in applying the new sculptural formalism; or perhaps their eyes turned more to the Scandinavian understatement of such architects as Sweden's Gunnar Asplund and Sven Markelius and Denmark's Arne Jacobsen. Ferguson & McIlveen's Members Rooms attached to the King's Hall at Balmoral, Belfast (1964) enhances the original building but keeps much of its structural daring in reserve behind a restrained and flat façade. St Columba's Church and Hall at Lisburn (1969) and Munce & Kennedy's Presbyterian Church, Harmony Hill, Lambeg are both neutral in tone, they turn inwards toward courtyard gardens and keep the world at a distance. The same restraint is evident in Patrick Haughey's Church of St Theresa, Sion Mills (1965) which handles the architecture of classical precedent with rigour and clarity. Liam McCormick's work, however, embraces the new order and his churches are loaded with multicultural references.

Belfast Airport at Aldergrove, designed by W.H. McAllister Armstrong and Partners and winner of an RIBA Award for the Ulster region in 1966, is an early expression of the new wave. Before its recent enlargement it was a scenographic tour-de-force, dramatic in its symbolism of flight, and crisp and legible in its organization and structure. The design team for the project included two young Scottish architects, Joe FitzGerald and Jim Kennedy whose careers enriched Ulster architecture. Both had trained at the School of Architecture at Dundee and arrived in Belfast in 1958 to work for the Northern Ireland Housing Trust after spending a year in the office of Gillespie Kidd & Coia in Glasgow. (There are strong historical links between Ulster and Scotland and many local architects trained at Scottish universities – and still do.) Ulster has always benefited from the arrival of new talents – Charles Lanyon, an Englishman, arrived here in the 1830s made Belfast his home and established the architectural profession here. FitzGerald and Kennedy too settled here and brought with them a high level of design and professionalism.

These two Scottish architects worked together as a design team between 1963 and 1984 and the selection of their buildings included in this book reflects their achievement although pressure of space has meant the exclusion of many notable projects. These include the Collegiate School, Enniskillen winner of an RIBA Award in 1969; the Model School, Enniskillen which received an RIBA Commendation in 1976; the Valley Leisure Centre, Newtownabbey winner of a British Steel Award in 1977; Fleming Fulton School, Belfast, recipient of an RIBA Commendation and *Ulster Architect's* Building of the Year Award in 1985; Antrim Technology Park (in various phases) which received an RIBA Commendation and *Ulster Architect's* Building of the Year Award in 1989; and St Brigid's Church, Belfast, winner of the UK Brick Award in 1996 and of RIBA and RIAI Awards in 1996. The practice also won the RIAI Triennial Award 1983-85 for Calvert House, Castle Place, Belfast. To none of these projects, nor those selected for the book, could New Brutalism be applied with any accuracy but they very much belong to the canons of Modernism as expounded by the Smithsons and they contain echoes of the work of the Modernist masters. A theme that characterises their projects is the skilful tailoring of the design to the cloth of the site, so that building and terrain act together and dialogues are set up between the enclosed spaces and the buildings that enclose them.

Most of the buildings included are the work of the generation of architects who had trained 'across the water' or had qualified externally through the RIBA. These include Robinson & McIlwaine, Ian Campbell & Partners, McCormick Tracey Mullarkey, Gordon McKnight and Rooney & McConville. From the 70s onward local graduates from Queen's University began to play a part in the province's architecture, represented by such firms as Todd Architects, Consarc Design Group, Hall Black Douglas, Mackel & Doherty, Box Architects, twenty two over seven and Kennedy FitzGerald & Associates.

The selection of works is partly based upon the RIBA Regional Awards – usually a fair indication of a building's merit as it is the assessment of an impartial peer group

2.11 – 2.13
Belfast Airport, Aldergrove
(RIBA Award 1966),
by W. H. McAllister
Armstrong and Partners
2.11 JOE FITZGERALD
2.12-2.13 HENK SNOEK / RIBA LIBRARY
PHOTOGRAPHS COLLECTION

2.14 – 2.15
Folk Life Gallery, Ulster Folk
and Transport Museum,
Cultra (RIBA Award 1983),
by Ferguson & McIlveen
CHRIS HILL

2.14 2.15

selected by the RIBA – and also upon the Ulster Architectural Heritage Society's view that these are examples of architectural design which will stand the test of time and, in the future, may be considered for listing. It is hoped that the buildings will be known, and referred to, by students of architecture as examples of innovative and influential design. It should be noted here that the Arts Council of Northern Ireland, as well as supporting this publication, has actively promoted Modernism in Ulster through its National Lottery Awards. The Market Place Theatre and Arts Centre in Armagh and the Arts, Cultural and Exhibition Centre in Strabane are notable instances of its patronage.

The book would be incomplete without some reference to Ferguson McIlveen's Folk Life Gallery at the Ulster Folk and Transport Museum. Behind the cool façades of profiled steel sheeting and glazed gables, the manipulation of the interior spaces around its winding ramp is a delight – a sequence of unfolding vistas and overlapping volumes make for a memorable marriage of circulation and gallery space. The Gallery received an RIBA Award in 1983. Other notable buildings by this long established and distinguished firm include Woodlands Presbyterian Church, Carrickfergus, winner of an RIBA Commendation in 1981 and the Research Laboratories at Magee which rise like a pair of silver shards from the wooded slopes of the campus.

The course of Modernism was well established in the 1970s when the first ripples of Postmodernism were first apparent; the term was coined by Charles Jencks, the American architect and critic, and in these islands it is associated with the collapse, in 1968, of Ronan Point, a tower block of flats in London. Modernism has long had its critics and they have never been short of ammunition; its professed internationalism suggesting a bland anonymity without regional flavour was confirmed by Corbusier's suggestion in 1937 that a single building type could suit all nations and climates. Its 'honesty' and lack of ornamentation smacked of Puritanism and its tough proletarian stance was responsible (to many eyes) for a joyless and colourless architecture.

2.16   2.17   2.18   2.19

Postmodernism, which was hailed as the demise of Modernism, was considered to be the way forward as it offered colour, pluralism and human interest. Architecture was to come out of the straightjacket and freedom of dress was to be the order of the day. Its rejection of the fundamentals of Modernism (that form follows function and the honest expression of structure) was a short-lived coup but it had some lasting repercussions. It spawned, in Peter Fawcett's words, 'the neo-vernacular of the 1970s, espousing apparently traditional methods and materials ... which was acceptable to client, developer and planner alike'. ('Planning permission vernacular' as Jonathan Glancey has described it). Its most memorable posture was the 'classicism' which 'debased architecture to an exercise in styling'.[18]

Ulster's most significant response to Postmodernism is Robinson & McIlwaine's General Accident Building, Donegall Square, Belfast, winner of an RIBA National Award in 1988. This distinguished building shows an educated use of classical precedents: the propylaeum entry and the implied 'pediments' of the attic storey. The building is a contextual response to the 'Wrenaissance' architecture of Belfast's City Hall.

Its critics will concede that Postmodernism brought contextualisation into the domain of design. It brought an ironic, or perhaps tentative, use of historical motifs to buildings in the urban setting. The legacy has been a degree of timidity in the design of infill projects which includes the makeover of existing frame buildings with mock Georgian façades. There has been, too, the dressing-up of new developments with heavy, arched brickwork façades, to recall the factory buildings of the Victorian city and its dark Titanic mills.

Contextualism at its best is evident in Mackel & Doherty's Bedeck Building, Lisburn Road, Belfast 2004. It maintains the kind of urbanism upon which the character of the city depends. Earlier examples of infill, such as Laurence McConville's Catholic

2.20   2.21

2.22

2.23   2.24

Chaplaincy in Elmwood Avenue, Belfast, and the Bank of Ireland, Donegall Place, Belfast by Kenneth Kiersey are modern in expression but they are very much at home in the streetscape through the virtues of appropriate scale and size. The infamous Northern Bank of 1970 in Donegall Square West is an excellent and relatively early example of good infill which brings a distinguished modern presence to the centre of Belfast. Its façades in Portland stone provide a severe counterpoint to its exuberant neighbour, Young & Mackenzie's Scottish Provident building of 1897-1902. Stokes House, College Square East, by Barrie Todd is another incidence of architecture that sacrifices none of its modernity in maintaining the integrity of the Georgian terrace which it extends.

Interventions of a more dramatic kind are seen in Robinson Patterson's Clarence Gallery, Linenhall Street, Belfast which received an RIBA Commendation in 1988; and in the Bar Library, Chichester Street, Belfast by Robinson & McIlwaine, winner of the Liam McCormick Prize 2004. The first offers a fully glazed gable to Linenhall Street as a Modernist counterpart to St Malachy's Church front as viewed along Clarence Street; the second, a gesture of civic grandeur and the panoply of the law. The play of receding masses, their shadows and the wide oversailing hipped roof bring incident and high drama to the cityscape and, within, the sequence of rich and varied interiors is detailed with finesse and precision.

The development of Modernism has been well documented over the last thirty years: *Ulster Architect*, edited by Anne Davey Orr, first appeared in 1984 and since then has maintained a lively commentary on the province's architecture. Many distinguished contributors to the journal have included Paul Larmour, Dick Oram, Andrew Cowser and Sir Charles Brett. Its Building of the Year Award scheme ran from 1985-1990. The Royal Society of Ulster Architect's journal *Perspective* has, since 1992, covered the major events in local architecture as well as the arts scene, and launched the Liam McCormick Prize in 1998. The Ulster Architectural Heritage Society's *Introduction*

2.25   2.26   2.27

to Modern Ulster Architecture[19] was the first survey of the local architecture of the post-war period and over the last half century a leading chronicler has been Robert McKinstry. He recorded the rise of Modernism in the post-war years in an extended essay published in *Causeway: the Arts in Ulster*, 1971 and in a series of articles written on the state of the profession in the 50s.[20] He has also written extensively on local architecture in the *Architects' Journal* and for the *RSUA Yearbook and Directory*. McKinstry was trained at Liverpool University School of Architecture, a contemporary of Henry Lynch Robinson and Liam McCormick, and after working in Paris and London he returned to Belfast in 1950. His career bridged Modernism and conservation; he worked extensively for the National Trust and was responsible for the interior remodelling of the RSUA headquarters, No. 1 Mount Charles, Belfast, following bomb damage in 1982. His refurbishment of the Grand Opera House, Belfast (with Melvyn Brown) won an RIBA Commendation in 1983. Writing in the *RSUA Yearbook* in the same year he confessed 'I find myself returning more and more, with ever increasing satisfaction to the calming order of a symmetrical arrangement and that perfect harmony between scale, proportion and materials found in, say, an early 19th century English Rectory'.[21] It reads like a valedictory note to Modernism but his design for the Visitors' Centre at Crawfordsburn Country Park in 1988 can not only, it seems, claim these virtues but in its clarity of form, expressive use of structure and materials also touches on Modernism and regional identity.

Today the lamp of Modernism in Ulster shines bright. It might have flickered in the last twenty years but it has emerged the stronger from a period of soul searching and the caprice of Postmodernism. It has recovered its nerve and there are signs of a return to 'good old-fashioned Modernism' tempered, however, by experience and more responsive to environmental issues and to both the urban and rural heritage. Ulster's buildings refer to memory, metaphor and historical allusion but they also perform better as human environments and are more energy efficient than their predecessors.

2.25
Clarence Gallery, Belfast
(RIBA commendation 1988),
by Robinson Patterson
MARK HACKETT 2005

2.26
The Bar Library, Belfast
(Liam McCormick Prize 2004),
by Robinson & McIlwaine
CHRIS HILL

2.27
Visitors' Centre, Crawfordsburn
Country Park (1988),
by Robert McKinstry
PHOTOGRAPH BY ARCHITECT

References

1 Introduction. In Longley, M. (ed). *Causeway: the arts in Ulster.* Belfast: The Arts Council of Northern Ireland, 1971. 8.

2 Brett, C.E.B. The duty of the architect towards Ulster's architectural heritage. *RSUA Yearbook and Directory, 1971.*

3 Esher, L.B. Canons of criticisms –2. *Architectural Review,* 109(651), 1951. 135-137.

4 Banham, R. *Theory and design in the first machine age.* Oxford: Butterworth-Heinemann Ltd, 1960.

5 Pevsner, N. *The sources of modern architecture and design.* London: Thames and Hudson, 1968.

6 ibid.

7 Hitchcock, H.R. *Architecture: nineteenth and twentieth centuries.* London: Yale University Press, 1987.

8 Esher, L.B. *A broken wave: the rebuilding of England 1940-1980.* London: Allen Lane, 1981.

9 Meek, H. Festival of Britain. In Hatje,G. (ed). *Encyclopaedia of modern architecture.* London: Thames & Hudson, 1963. 98.

10 The exhibition as a town builders pattern book. *Architectural Review,* 110 (656), 1951. 107-122.

11 Brooks, L.K. *The Festival of Britain in Ulster.* Queen's University Belfast, School of Architecture dissertation, 1990.

12 Hanna, D O'D. Architecture in Ulster. In Bell, S.H., Robb, N.A. and Hewitt, J. (eds). *The arts in Ulster: a symposium.* London: George G. Harrap & Co. Ltd, 1951. 25-44.

13 *Foreword to British architects' conference.* Belfast: Nicholson & Bass, 1951.

14 *Report on the Arts festival in Northern Ireland organised by CEMA.* Belfast: CEMA, 1952.

15 The Festival of Britain exhibitions review. *Architectural Review,* 110(657),1952. 192.

16 McKinstry, R. Contemporary architecture. In Longley, M. (ed). *Causeway: the arts in Ulster.* Belfast: The Arts Council of Northern Ireland, 1971. 27-37.

17 ibid.

18 Fawcett, P. The death of postmodernism. In *RSUA Yearbook and Directory.* Belfast: RSUA, 1990. 100-101

19 Evans, D. *An introduction to modern Ulster architecture.* Belfast: UAHS,1977.

20 McKinstry, R. 1971. op.cit.

21 McKinstry, R. Some ideas on artchitecture (sic). In *RSUA Yearbook and Directory.* Belfast: RSUA, 1983.

PART ONE

ESSAY THREE CHARLES RATTRAY

Ulster Modernism: an outside view

CHARLES RATTRAY

Ulster can be a confusing term. It is the name of an ancient Irish province and is also often used to refer to the area more correctly known as Northern Ireland. John Montague called it a 'history-burdened area, the North'.[1] His fellow-poet Louis MacNeice put it with characteristic satire: 'God save – as you prefer – the King or Ireland'.[2] If many of Ulster's place-names suggest a gentle continuity – Drumena, Cashel, Ballycastle, Malin Head – others form a no less evocative catalogue and live on in the imaginations of people who have never visited them; such was the power of news reports of the Troubles.

This book, in accordance with the aims of its publisher, covers the nine counties of Ulster. It reflects the fact that the gravitational pull of architectural culture in Ireland – the schools of architecture, the concentration of practice – is shared between Dublin and Belfast. The wider scope is refreshing, too.

Firstly because this book is concerned only with very good architecture – and architecture of that sort is always concerned with issues that lie beyond boundaries, such as tradition, technology, expression and our relations with nature and ourselves. Secondly because at the same time it implies that the roots of an architecture that might reflect a regional culture grow in what Juhani Pallasmaa has described as 'the spiritual soil, the frame of reference and understanding'.[3]

In describing modern architecture in Ulster as it has been developed and challenged in particular circumstances, in relation to a particular place, this book also enters into an area that has a mixed history in Modernism. Only in the last twenty-five years has there been any noticeable international interest in regionalism in contemporary architecture. You don't have to be an aficionado to take a special interest in this. In fact those cynical about the utopian ideals of the 'new' architecture of the 1920s have rejoiced in the passing of the so-called International Style, as Hitchcock and Johnson described the modern work of those times.[4] Hitchcock and Johnson's book, first

3.0 – 3.1
Weekend House,
Muuratsalo, Finland (1952-4),
by Alvar Aalto.
CHARLES RATTRAY

3.0   3.1

published in 1932, has been much criticised for its preoccupation with solely stylistic criteria for the buildings it included (the very mention of it is guaranteed to raise the hackles of many architects). But, whatever one thinks of it, their title does tell a certain truth: an important legacy of early Modernism was a lack of interest in the uniqueness and specifics of place.

Part of this was a result of the (by present day standards, innocent) pressures of publication and dissemination. They nurture the compelling pleasures of abstraction – of the two-dimensional plan and section, say, or the iconic photograph. Many such mesmeric images provide elegant testimony for disconnection. Part of this, too, was the work itself. We might set to one side the loveable curiosity of Le Corbusier's house for his parents on Lake Geneva, built in 1923-4. This started life as a plan without a plot: 'With the plan in our pockets' he wrote 'we spent a long time looking for a site'.[5] Rather we might consider his prismatic Villa Savoie near Paris, completed in 1931. Here the structural columns (pilotis) touch the ground lightly around an entrance floor determined by the turning-circle of a Citroën. It was the influential high point of Le Corbusier's purism but it had little to say about place; almost immediately after completing it, his work moved to a more substantive and site-specific architecture exemplified by the Weekend House of 1935.

Even in such more rooted work, however, contextual attitudes derive as much from wider culture as from specific location. Take, for example, Alvar Aalto's 1953 summerhouse at Muuratsalo. His drawn studies of the immediate surroundings describe a special sensitivity to place that is borne out as you approach the house along a tramped footpath in the berry-laden field-layer of the forest. Gaps between the trees begin to reveal outbuildings, which make an informal court in conjunction with the natural landform. Beyond that, however, the house itself, with its walled courtyard horizontal against the falling contours, speaks as much of Imperial Rome as of rural Finland.

The positive side of this sort of dislocation is shown clearly by an extreme example. William Curtis has described Mies van der Rohe's Farnsworth House of 1946 as 'supremely anti-natural [...] the obverse of Wright's landscape Romanticism'.[6] It is a comparison that reminds us that there were Modern architects who were deeply interested in the specifics of place (other examples being Dmitris Pikionis and Carlo Scarpa), yet in the case of Mies' great work, which is as foreign to the land as a recently alighted helicopter, it is precisely the elegance of the contrast that engenders a frisson of delight.

In the relationship of technology to Modernism similar difficulties with locality and local tradition arise. One can point to an early divorce from local building materials as architects first began to employ an extensive range of factory-produced materials and components after the First World War. It was the end of the vernacular tradition and the way in which humble buildings would reflect the geology or tradition of their location. There were important changes in the way materials were assembled, too. The developing interest in the *promenade architecturale* and in complex subdivisions within cubic volumes prompted the elimination of detail that was not essential to spatial understanding. As walls became free-standing planes, for example, then the traditional skirting board became an embarrassment (it conveniently makes good the junction between wall and floor but inconveniently continues around corners). It had to go. For a joiner its loss, and replacement by a shadow-gap, was awkward and counter-intuitive.

Much of the recent interest in regionalism in architecture has less to do with any nostalgia for these lost traditions and more to do with an equally romantic longing for some sort of 'cultural essence' that has been hidden or smothered by that universal technology.[7] Hugh Dixon makes a typical lament: 'too many buildings erected in Ulster during the first three-quarters of the 20th century have ignored ... specifically Ulster characteristics. In their pursuit of international fashions some architects have overlooked the traditional local qualities.'[8] This is ironic – or at least nothing new – given that Dixon comments on an early 17th-century plantation castle (Ballygally in Antrim) that 'it might as well have been built in Greenock'.[9] In our own times, however, it is because of that sort of reaction to a universal culture that Kenneth Frampton's famous essay entitled 'Towards a Critical Regionalism' is subtitled 'Six Points for an Architecture of Resistance'.[10]

Alan Colquhoun presents a more conciliatory, or more nuanced, reading of all this, arguing that 'It is precisely because the ingredients of contemporary architecture are so similar all over the 'developed' world that the slight differences of interpretation to which they are subjected in different countries becomes so interesting. [...] Their areas of demarcation are the most obvious and banal divisions of the modern political world [...] it is regionalism based on politics.'[11]

For Ulster, such a regionalism seems especially clear: a truism perhaps. Consider these remarks 'The year in which Aalto launched his career [...] was a remarkable year: 1922. It was, for instance, the year in which Joyce's *Ulysses*, Eliot's *The Wasteland* and Wittgenstein's *Tractatus* were published, and Le Corbusier's *Vers une architecture* was completed; Mies van der Rohe had just produced his most astonishing vision of the glass tower, and Le Corbusier his project for a contemporary city for 3,000,000 people. It was indeed the year in which Corb himself set up his practice in Paris, and it was the year adopted by Barr, Hitchcock and Johnson as the birth of the International Style.'[12] It was also the time of the creation of Northern Ireland.

This new state (and its Ulster neighbours, Donegal, Cavan and Monaghan) was 'building on the edge of Europe', as a book title has it[13] and also on the edge of the UK and on the edge of independent Ireland. Are aspects of this environment reflected and revealed in the work? Are key moments in its recent history evoked in the buildings and townscape?

On the ground, some cross-cultural aspects are very obvious: you don't need border controls to notice the changing petrol prices and, more recently, the arrival of the euro. But even from an aeroplane – especially from an aeroplane – the green-belt inheritance of the UK's post-war planning system contrasts strongly with the Republic's ribbon development of houses – almost all assisted by publication of house plan pattern books. The most famous of these, *Bungalow Bliss*, is punned mischievously as 'bungalow blitz' and 'bungalow blight'.[14] Frank McDonald argues that its success is part of the 'cult of rabid individualism that is very much part of Ireland's post-colonial psyche';[15] Shane O'Toole describes the result 'a chaotic scrawl … which we Irish have scribbled all over much of our dishevelled landscape'.[16] It is certainly a vigorous revival of notions of homestead in a newly dynamic economy.

In Northern Ireland, one senses a different culture, with or without planning rules. There has sometimes been evidence of an uneasy balance for architecture: in the Republic of Ireland, De Valera's innate conservatism; in Northern Ireland, the depression of a post-war economy. Sometimes, too, there has been a clear imbalance: the boom known as the 'Celtic Tiger' transformed the Republic's fortunes as it embraced a European context while Northern Ireland remained a political hot spot from which many young architects escaped to London or to Dublin.

When the Smithsons delineated 'The Heroic Period of Modern Architecture' of 1910-1937 for *Architectural Design* in 1965, they did so by choosing 150 or so buildings and projects.[17] The Smithsons' organisation was by date, but the concentration of that work by countries is interesting and very focused. In The Netherlands, the clarity and conviction of pre-war architecture was demonstrated in work such as Brinkman and Van der Vlugt's Van Nelle factory, Duiker's Open Air School and work by Mart Stamm and J J P Oud. France had the advantage of Swiss-born Le Corbusier, whose prodigious output accounts for all of their entries apart from Chareau's *Maison de verre*. The Soviet Union's examples are the Constructivists. There is little else. Surprising,

3.2
St Peter's Church,
Milford, Co Donegal (1966),
by F. Corr and
W.H.D. McCormick.
MARK HACKETT 2005

3.3
Convent Chapel, Cookstown,
(1963),
by Laurence McConville.
MARK HACKETT 2005

3.4
Ulster Museum Extension,
Belfast (1965),
by Francis Pyn.
MARK HACKETT 2005

3.2   3.3   3.4

from a present-day perspective, is the very limited showing of Spain and Switzerland
– countries whose architects are much celebrated now. Then there are one or two
buildings from the UK, but nothing from Ulster. The only works that would have
fitted within the Smithsons' intention and time-scale are Hugh Gault's houses in
Belfast of the mid-30s.[18] They are almost the only Ulster architecture of the 20s and
30s that neither harked back to 19th-century Classicism nor fell victim to Art Deco.
Nevertheless, in the Heroic context they can be seen only as followers of the avant-
garde and not contributors to it. Gault might have consoled himself with the thought
that the Smithsons did not include work by Aalto either.

A year later, the *Architects' Journal* published 'An Irish Appetiser' to that year's RIBA
conference in Dublin.[19] This turned out to be a not entirely unusual combination
of Celtic nostalgia, enthusiasm and condescension. It was much preoccupied by the
urgency for a coherent city plan for Dublin and mesmerised by Georgian decoration
(at a convent on Dublin's Henrietta Street, 'the nuns not only do untold work in a
desperately poor district but maintain the plaster work with great care'). It was rather
less impressed by Modern work. 'The less said about new buildings the better', wrote
Ian Nairn – a view evidently shared by the editors who presented a curious round-up
of buildings nominated by Irish architects themselves while pleading that 'It was
not possible for the AJ to visit all the architects in Ireland...' From Ulster, there were
four schemes: offices for the Pigs Marketing Board, by Munce and Kennedy; Corr and
McCormick's early St Peter's Church at Milford, Co. Donegal; the conversion work
for the Ulster Folk Museum by Ian Campbell; and – a real period-piece, this – the cubic
concrete extension of Laurence McConville's 1963 Convent Chapel at Cookstown,
Co. Tyrone (p.62).

One can immediately think of a further four buildings that ought to have been included
in any coherent survey of the time. Francis Pym's sculptural Ulster Museum of 1965
(p.64) is a much more sophisticated variant of the concrete-box-extension theme

3.5   3.6   3.7   3.8   3.9

that was surely unmissable. Similarly, for a distinguished journal not to have uncovered the almost Californian houses of Noel Campbell (p.52) or the spatial and material pleasures of the Ashby Institute at Queen's of 1964 (p.56) was an editorial disgrace. Patrick Haughey's very controlled St. Theresa's church at Sion Mills was left out too. This is perhaps an architect's architecture: a Grecian austerity offset by the seductive use of south light to make abstract patterns from pews and their shadows and to throw into relief the texture of the rough limestone wall behind the altar.

The decades following the 60s are the immediate background to our own time. Here, one of the many pleasant surprises in this book is the number of buildings that date from the 1970s – the height of the Troubles. The obvious demands of security in Northern Ireland and their effect on buildings and places have been well summarised by Stollard.[20] In response one would surely have expected a sort of architectural Dark Age in Northern Ireland with young architects leaving and clients adopting a protective stance. But the work of Shanks Leighton Kennedy FitzGerald in particular (admittedly in publicly funded commissions) (p.88 and 96) shows extraordinary vigour and optimism while Liam McCormick's remarkable series of churches on both sides of the border (at Creeslough p.82, Glenties p.92 and Steelstown p.94) deserve a book of their own.

On the other hand, the few projects from the 1980s in these pages hint at more difficult times. Increased political co-operation between Dublin and London made little change on the ground and the lack of confidence in any resolution to the Troubles inevitably slowed investment in buildings. At the same time, for Northern Ireland as for the rest of the UK, the Thatcher government's policies applied. This meant open competition in architects' fees, more design and build and the advent of private finance initiatives in public work. In the Republic of Ireland, by contrast, there was an early embrace of the European Union rule on competitive interviews for public projects where fees were discussed only after a practice was selected.

3.10   3.11   3.12   3.13   3.14

In recent years Ulster's Modernism – and implicit in this are also reactions to Modernism – has shown a considerable variety. The evidence in this book shows that this was not produced at the expense of quality. Of course the role of the authors here has been difficult: where to draw the line? It is like choosing how to contain a list of wedding guests. If second cousin Jean is invited, then all the other remote cousins must be asked too. Inclusiveness, then, is definitely not the issue here. Rather it is a critical discrimination.

My mentor Leslie Martin put it very well when he said that 'distinctions between the works of great architects are interesting, but these divisions do not occur to me as the important ones. If I drew any line at all, the line which I would draw would be horizontal and not vertical. Above this horizontal line I would choose to place the work of these great designers, and below it the rest'.[21]

Four contrasting schemes within these pages demonstrate Martin's point. The Falls Road Leisure Centre by Kennedy FitzGerald and Associates (p.158) is an example of a classic developed Modernism. The technical and programmatic requirements are resolved with a complete assurance that then allows a full exploration of expressive possibilities. The clarity of the internal organisation, varying in height under a constant roof level, is emphasised by its internal transparency. Externally, too, transparency, light and colour take on a positive and transformative role in its very difficult context.

Entirely different is Liam McCormick's church at Creeslough (p.82). This is strikingly allusive. The sculpted monumentality of its massive walls takes the dramatic scenery of the Muckish Mountains beyond and re-presents it to you as you approach. The building helps you to see the place. Internally, one clearly framed opening objectifies the mountains while other windows – to the side-chapel – borrow from Le Corbusier's church at Ronchamp. It is a tribute to the architect that a gesture like that, which could so easily be seen as trivial, here seems no more than an entirely appropriate homage.

3.15   3.16   3.17

A narrative quality distinguishes MacGabhann Architects' extraordinary council offices at Letterkenny (p.140). This is a hugely competent and characterful building of international quality built in a small town on the fringe of Europe. In this sense it recalls Alvar Aalto's famous town hall for Säynätsalo, a rural place with a population of 3,000. Tarla and Antoin MacGabhann are locals who have taken on their father's architectural practice. Tarla's formative architectural experience has been with the Polish-born Jewish-American, Daniel Libeskind, working in Berlin. It is one thing to come from a place; it is another to return and bring a cosmopolitan analysis to a deeply familiar situation.

Both McCormick's church and MacGabhann's offices represent the beginnings of a critical reappraisal of context in Ulster. In doing this they also reflect a wider freedom which has entered recent Modern architecture. As Functionalism has come to be seen as a myth, or a conceit, architecture has been freed to embrace the fragmentary and allusive qualities so essential to Modern art in general and so strikingly evident in *Ulysses* and *The Wasteland* specifically.[22] This is grown-up architecture visible again at Alan Jones's recently completed house in Randalstown (p.156). Here the pitched roof and dark finish appear on one level to be conventional usages but on another as catalysts for new associations. The interior is a surprise. Jones himself comments that it is 'as if the formalist tray has been shaken'.[23] The result is a spatial intrigue, 'a Trojan horse whose acceptable exterior hides other less expected meanings'.[24]

The contexts of Alan Jones's house include Randalstown but are also pan-European and intellectually diverse. This is a sign of a modern Ulster, no longer 'on the edge' but connecting with the wide world beyond. This book reflects such optimism. It focuses on the best of Ulster architecture, a subject that – as often poignantly as inspiringly – places confidence in the future.

3.15 – 3.16
Letterkenny Council Offices (2002),
by MacGabhann Architects.
MARK HACKETT 2005

3.17
Architect's Own House,
Randalstown (2005),
by Alan Jones.
PHOTOGRAPH BY ARCHITECT 2005

References

1 Montague, J. In the Irish grain. In Montague, J. (ed). *The Faber Book of Irish Verse*. London: Faber and Faber, 1974. 37.

2 MacNeice, L. *Autumn Journal*, xvi, 1939. 32.

3 Pallasmaa, J. The world made flesh. In *alt'ing*, 1(1), 1996. 76.

4 Hitchcock, H-R., and Johnson, P. *The International Style*. New York: Norton, 1995.

5 Le Corbusier. *Une petite maison*. Basel: Birkhäuser, 2001. 7.

6 Curtis, W. *Modern architecture since 1900*. London: Phaidon Press, 1987. 262.

7 Colquhoun, A. *Modernity and the Classical tradition*. Cambridge, MA: MIT Press, 1989. 208.

8 Dixon, H. *An introduction to Ulster architecture*. Belfast: Ulster Architectural Heritage Society, 1975. vii.

9 ibid. 22.

10 Frampton, K. Towards a critical regionalism: six points for an architecture of resistance. In Foster, H. (ed). *The anti-aesthetic: essays on Postmodern culture*. Seattle: Bay Press, 1983. 16-31.

11 Colquhoun, A. op cit. 208.

12 St. John Wilson, C. *Architectural reflections: studies in the philosophy and practice of architecture*. Oxford: Butterworth Architecture, 1992.

13 Graby, J. (ed). *Building on the edge of Europe*. Dublin: Royal Institute of the Architects of Ireland, 1996.

14 Fitzsimons, J. *Bungalow bliss*. 6th ed. Kells, Kells Art Studios, 1976.

15 McDonald, F. Ireland's suburbs. In Becker, A. , Olley, J. and Wang. W. (eds). *20th century architecture : Ireland*. Munich & New York: Prestel Verlag, 1997. 50.

16 O'Toole, S. On marked and abandoned ground. *A+U*, (397), 2003. 112.

17 Smithson, A. and Smithson, P. The heroic period of Modern architecture. *Architectural Design*, 35 (12), 1965. 590-639.

18 Larmour, P. *Belfast : an illustrated architectural guide*. Belfast: Friar's Bush Press, 1987. 90.

19 An Irish appetiser. *Architects' Journal*, 144 (10), 1966. 565ff.

20 Stollard, P. The architecture of no man's land. *Architects' Journal*, 180 (31), 1984. 24-39.

21 Martin, L. Introduction to the 1957 RIBA Discourse by Alvar Aalto. *RIBA Journal*, 64 (7), 1957. 258.

22 Private communication from Bob Maxwell.

23 Private communication from Alan Jones.

24 MacCormac, R. Housing and the dilemma of style. *Architectural Review*, 163 (974), 1978. 202-206.

PART TWO

BUILDINGS

Orangefield Presbyterian Church

BELFAST
GORDON McKNIGHT 1955–7

Churches were the last building type in the field of architecture in Ulster to succumb to Modernism, with historic style revivalism continuing into the post-war period. Symbolic form being such an important element in ecclesiastical design generally, and Ulster society in particular being so conservative, it is hardly surprising that traditional values, shapes and materials were retained for so long here even when every other building type had taken on a new and modern image.

In the church building world even comparatively modest or superficial change was considered significant. Thus Orangefield Presbyterian Church, a

relatively traditional design, built of rustic brick with a steep-pitch slated roof and an attached belfry tower, carried enough unusual details for the local press to describe it as 'built to the most modern design'.

The earlier and smaller gabled pre-war church hall to the east probably gave the cue for the general shape of this post-war church designed by Gordon McKnight but the treatment of detail is clearly 'Festival of Britain' inspired, from the segmental canopy roof of the tower with its copper spike-and-ball finial, to the skewered-ball side window balcony railings and front gates. The tall and attenuated porch projecting from the entrance main gable,

with its doorway set in a large expanse of glazing and green slates, is also entirely of the period, drawing ecclesiastical design into the new world of curtain glazing and panel systems.

Inside, the main interior is like a lecture room, with a raking floor which slopes down toward the sanctuary area in which there is a central pulpit reached by short twin flights of steps, the woodwork and tubular metal supports of which are all detailed in a crisp modern style which is also reflected in the lines and form of the pew ends. This almost entirely unspoiled example of 1950s architecture marked the start of McKnight's long career as a

References

Orangefield Presbyterian Church. *Belfast News-Letter*, 7 September 1957.

New buildings in North and South. *Irish Builder and Engineer*, 12 July 1958. 503.

The Presbyterian Church in Ireland. *Church building in the Presbyterian Church in Ireland 1950-1962*. Belfast, 1962. 19-20.

Larmour, P. *Belfast: an illustrated architectural guide*. Belfast: Friar's Bush Press, 1987. 97.

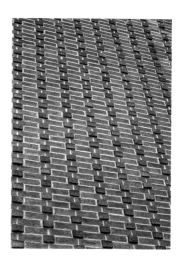

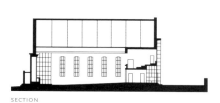

SECTION

SIDE ELEVATION

FRONT ELEVATION

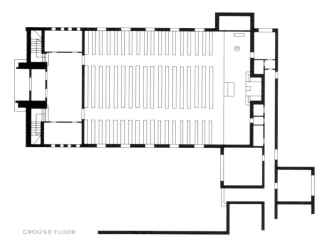

GROUND FLOOR

0 ⊢————————— 10

specialist designer which saw him build over thirty churches for Protestant denominations during the course of four decades. They include Orangefield Baptist Church, Belfast (1968), Methodist College Chapel, Belfast (1968), St Columba's Church of Ireland, Portadown (1970), St Andrew and Knockbreda Combined Church, Belfast (1971), High Kirk, Ballymena (1976), Corrymeela Worship Centre, Ballycastle (1978-9), and Albertbridge Road Congregational Church, Belfast (1985-6).

More uncompromisingly modern churches for Protestant worship were designed in the early 1960s by the likes of W McK Davidson, at West Presbyterian Church, Bangor,

Co Down (1962); Shanks and Leighton, at the Queen's University Church of Ireland Students' Centre in Elmwood Avenue, Belfast (1963-4); and Munce and Kennedy, at Harmony Hill Presbyterian Church, Lambeg (1966), but it was McKnight's particular blend of tradition and modernity, often wrought in romantic vein, which proved most popular in Ulster.

Scandia

BALLYMENA   CO ANTRIM
NOEL CAMPBELL   1959–60

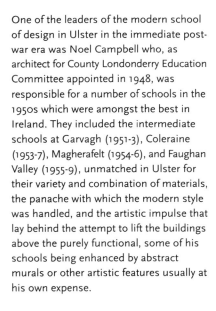

One of the leaders of the modern school of design in Ulster in the immediate post-war era was Noel Campbell who, as architect for County Londonderry Education Committee appointed in 1948, was responsible for a number of schools in the 1950s which were amongst the best in Ireland. They included the intermediate schools at Garvagh (1951-3), Coleraine (1953-7), Magherafelt (1954-6), and Faughan Valley (1955-9), unmatched in Ulster for their variety and combination of materials, the panache with which the modern style was handled, and the artistic impulse that lay behind the attempt to lift the buildings above the purely functional, some of his schools being enhanced by abstract murals or other artistic features usually at his own expense.

His growing reputation as a young go-ahead designer led inevitably to a number of private house commissions, culminating in a notable series of very avant-garde designs in the late 1950s and early 1960s which broke new ground in domestic architecture in Ulster. They included the partially cantilevered Rainey House of 1958-9 at Dhu Varren, Portrush, Co Antrim, the almost equally eye-catching Smyth House, also of 1958, with its unusual butterfly roof, at Strand Road, Portstewart, Co Londonderry, and the split level 'Little Rock' at Larkhilll Road, Portstewart, of around 1960.

The most interesting of the series, and the most accomplished example of a house in the International Style in Ulster, is 'Scandia', at Brocklamont Park in Ballymena, Co Antrim, built as a family house in 1959-60 for a local businessman John Lee, a director of the Braidwater Spinning Company. A single-storey house laid out on an asymmetrical plan with a cruciform arrangement of overlapping flat roofs, its slick form and sophisticated detailing owes much to the example of Richard Neutra in America in the late 1940s, and something also to Mies van der Rohe, with its all glass walls around the lounge and dining area, detailed with such precision that the floor and roof planes can pass from inside to outside without interruption. Superb corner glazing details, unique for a house in Ireland at the time, accentuate the abstract qualities of the composition, as does the highly polished finish of the terrazzo paving around the all-glass bay.

The view from the house looks out to beautifully landscaped gardens in front, and over a large terrace to one side which originally incorporated a swimming pool (later converted to a patio garden), its enclosing walls decorated with mosaic

References

Evans, D. *An introduction to modern Ulster architecture.* Belfast: UAHS, 1977. 76.

Larmour, P. Scandia. In Becker, A. Olley, J. and Wang, W. (eds). *20th century architecture: Ireland.* Munich and New York: Prestel, 1997. 122.

Larmour, P. Style master. *Perspective,*5 (6),1997. 18-31.

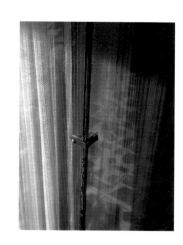

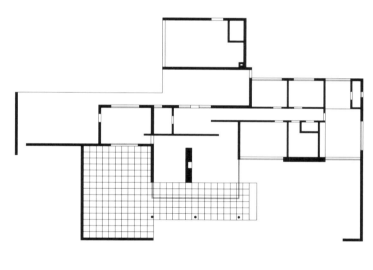

FLOOR PLAN   0 └─────────────┘ 10

murals of abstract patterns and female figures which appear to be swimming and playing with beach balls. These were designed and executed by the well-known Ulster artist Colin Middleton who was a friend of Campbell and who was at that time teaching at Coleraine Technical School. Another local Ulster artist, the sculptor James McKendrie, was commissioned by Campbell to design and execute the large abstract copper sculpture which stands on a low podium in the front lawn terminating a low wall projecting from the end of the house.

The architect's inventive approach to design, and richness of detail, was also carried through to the interior of the house, where a miniature cascade of water was designed to flow down the full height of the polished black marble face of a free-standing rubble stone partition containing

a fireplace in the lounge and thereby prevent the centrally-heated atmosphere from becoming too dry. The water fell into a small tank set beneath floor level. The walls of the lounge and hallway were covered with Corbusier-design wallpapers.

Essentially a composition of planes and enclosures in its original form, the building has undergone some changes over the past few decades. Accommodation has now been extended into the former yard and new rooms and another entrance thereby created; the originally open covered entrance between the house and the garage has now been partially closed in; and the garage itself extended. These later extensions, not by the original architect, have been carried out in a visually sympathetic manner but have inevitably diminished the original spatial complexity. One small later alteration which has

adversely affected the appearance of the house on the garden side is the insertion of a circular 'porthole' window in the rubble stone wall, a period motif which was already out of date when the house was first designed, and now detracts from the almost timeless and serene abstraction of Campbell's initial creation.

Outlook

HOLYWOOD CO DOWN
IAN CAMPBELL 1959–92

Whereas the main influence on Noel Campbell's luxurious houses of the 1950s and 60s was North American, the inspiration for the house which his brother Ian Campbell designed for himself in 1959 was Scandinavian. 'Outlook', which stands in a pleasantly wooded site, in a setting of mature larch, oak, and pine, sloping gently down towards the south shore of Belfast Lough, is testimony to its architect's particular admiration for the work of the Finnish master Alvar Aalto, in its generous timberwork and steeply monopitched forms, and his own sensitive and painstaking approach to design. The house has grown with the changing needs of the family, and has been extended several times, but it still retains the charm and the essential simplicity of the original concept. It consists of two blocks placed at right antgles to each other and linked by a glazed recessed porch, one of the blocks containing mainly sleeping accommodation, while the other contains the living accommodation. The clear functionality of this simple layout is given distinctly modern yet appropriately modest expression in its juxtaposition of flat-roofed and monopitched forms, and its choice of simple materials, comprising traditional white roughcast walls on a natural stone plinth with stained timber windows and panels. To the rear of the house lies the original paved terrace, incorporating a long narrow ornamental pool with a border of pebbles along the rear wall.

A later extension saw the single-storey bedroom block raised a floor, with the introduction of clerestory glazing, but the original form of the walls was retained by allowing the line of the original roof to dictate the design of the gable-end windows. Later still, in 1976, the living room block which contained a workroom in its loft at the front, a development of an Irish vernacular feature, was extended to one end with the conversion of the original

References

House in Belfast, Northern Ireland. *Architectural Design*, 32(3),1962. 137.

A house above Belfast Lough. *House and Garden*, 20 (7), 1965. 46-47.

Evans, D. *An introduction to modern Ulster architecture*. Belfast: UAHS, 1977. 81-82.

The house that goes on growing. *House and Garden*, 33(7), 1978. 116-117.

A touch of glass. *Perspective*, 3(3),1995. 47-48.

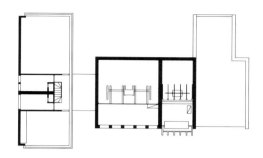

FIRST FLOOR

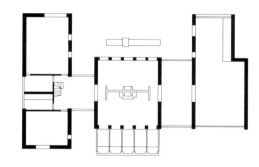

GROUND FLOOR

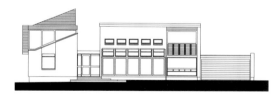

ELEVATION   0 |_____| 10

carport into a new kitchen, again with a loft at the front, and a new garage added onto the end. More recently, in 1992, a glazed summer room was added onto the west facing living room wall enclosing the five original floor-to-ceiling window openings which then became an open colonnade inside.

Throughout the interior, the architect's love of pine is evident, in walls and ceilings of diagonal sheeting in the bedroom block, exposed pine rafters and beams in the living room block, and large double-width pivoting pine doors which separate the inter-linked living and dining areas from

the entrance hall and the kitchen. In a further contrast to the purity of white plastered walls, the central chimney of the living room is flanked by screen walls of exposed yellow fire-brick. Because the house is an architect's own home, an unusual unity has always existed between building and furniture, with ingenious fittings and fixtures designed by Campbell himself, complemented by some well chosen classics of modern design by Aalto and others.

Long recognised as an architectural purist, Ian Campbell has produced work which has been marked for over forty years by its

neatness of planning, ingenuity of structure, refinement of form, and delightful attention to detail. These qualities can be seen in varying degrees in such works of the 1960s as the extension to Cultra Manor at the Ulster Folk Museum (1963, with Robert McKinstry), Dundonald Methodist Church (1967-9, with Artek), and Fanum House in Belfast (1966-8).

Ashby Institute
Queen's University Belfast

BELFAST
CRUICKSHANK & SEWARD   1960–5

Grand in scale and in conception, the Ashby Institute dominates the skyline of south Belfast. If the University's intention was to establish an emphatic presence on Stranmillis Road (or as one wag put it, to build an empire upon which the sun shall never set), it has certainly succeeded. In some lights, however, the Ashby's white mass can seem almost spectral and on occasion by evening light it becomes a soft wash of pink against the sky. The site is marked as a sand pit on the Ordnance Survey of 1832-3, and subsequent excavations had cut a relatively flat area into the ground which rises from the Malone Road towards Stranmillis where the edge is now defined by a high retaining

wall. To the south, the ground rises towards Chlorine Gardens. The disposition of three separate blocks on this awkward site is clear and decisive in its ordering of form and function. Two low blocks, the heavy engineering laboratories and the lecture room, settle comfortably into the low ground level and the eleven-storey teaching block rises between them. The principal pedestrian access to the building is at first floor level on the Stranmillis Road and service access is from the Malone Road side at ground level.

The building belongs to the International Style which had become widespread in the years following the Second World War.

It is white, planar and its cubic forms are generally severe and lack curvilinear incident. The influence of Le Corbusier was an element of the style and the Ashby Institute can be seen as an adaptation of some Corbusian themes of both his early phase and his post-war work. The Engineering block recalls the smooth white façades and strip windows of his pre-war Purist villas and the prominent roof forms, cubes and cylinders are further instances. The building has an air of casual grandeur, the play of light and shade make for a sculptural event that hints of wider experiences than the Schools of Mechanical and Manufacturing Engineering perhaps have to offer. It looks the perfect

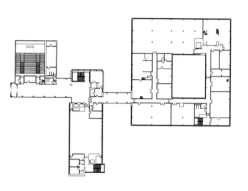

FIRST FLOOR PLAN

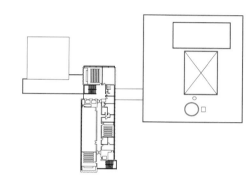

THIRD FLOOR PLAN

0 |_____| 10

FOURTH FLOOR PLAN

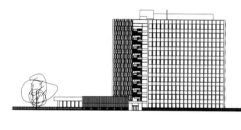

FLOOR PLAN

home for a collection of the avant-garde art of the 20s and 30s or the abstract expressionism of the New York School.

The teaching block seems to owe something to the Unité d'Habitation Marseilles, of 1947-52, in its form, the organisation of the façades and its north south alignment. It is a cool northern, even glacial version of the original, it has none of the stereometric power or colour; it is flat and neutral. Some sculptural incident comes with faceted diamond patterned panels which animate the long façades at the south end and also beside the staircase on the north elevation. (It has been suggested that this motif is a reference to the diamond paned windows of the Lanyon Building – a pleasant thought but without any substantiation.) There is a token reference to great pilotis which raise the Marseilles Unité clear of the ground; here the ground floor is not open space but the main structural columns are expressed and the interval between them is Mourne granite panelling, to differentiate the ground floor level from the main façade.

A two-storey glazed link connects the blocks. It starts with a cantilevered canopy and bridge which forms the Stranmillis Road entrance. It is a wide gallery like a promenade deck with full height glazing and hardwood strip flooring; it is a multi-functional space which takes up the slack in an otherwise rigidly defined sequence of spaces. More than a connecting element it is a concourse, a foyer to the auditorium, a social space and a venue for exhibitions. It represents the heart of the building. The refectory is situated below.

The concourse leads to the lift lobby and staircase in the teaching block, this is lined in 'knuckle' boarding in mahogany which has now taken on the vintage look of 60s architecture. The floor treatment of the entrance link carries through into this area which, with its completely glazed façade, can be seen as its vertical extension. The main stairway, as well as

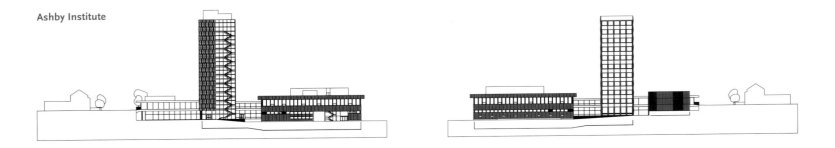

the secondary stair which leads down to the refectory, is now enclosed in glazed screens; health and safety regulations have meant that stairwells must be protected but something of the spatial flow and sense of continuity that was an important aspect of the original scheme has been sacrificed.

The junctions between forms, and the manner in which they engage, concern architects and here the meeting of the concourse link and the vertical glazing of the stairwell is clean and decisive. The short link to the Engineering block is almost tenuous, it barely impinges as it slides beneath the projection of the cantilevered

roof. This apparent disengagement as a means of handling functions is paralleled in small detail too. The circular columns, whose circumference is made up of flat planes, are protected at ground level by a circular steel collar which is projected clear of both the floor and the column face – an elementarist device to define the function of elements by separating them. (Few of these steel collars survive, alas.) The staircases again show this stylistic convention, treads and risers are a continuous folded plane in concrete, with terrazzo finish, that does not touch the timber-boarded walls nor the planes of glass that enclose them, but stands free,

carried by the raking beams of in situ reinforced concrete.

This building is a celebration of the use of reinforced concrete; its whiteness derives from the use of carboniferous limestone, quarried at Glenarm, for the aggregate. This stone is relatively soft and porous and there have been problems with spalling and the exposure of reinforcement but these difficulties have been rectified and the exterior has been sealed, otherwise the building has seemed impervious to the passing years. Although car parking has encroached upon the important green spaces surrounding it – the loss of the

References

Evans, D. and Larmour, P. *Queen's: an architectural legacy.* Belfast: Queen's University Institute of Irish Studies, 1995.

0 |___| 10

lawn beside the refectory is particularly regrettable – the building stands today as a pristine example of the architecture of the 60s and represents the best of it.

The apparent lack of concern with context is very much of its time. The building sits oddly among the small red brick terraces of Stranmillis, and as L.P. Hartley has it, 'the past is a different country they do things differently there'. The 60s seemed to many architects the dawn of a bright new world that would see the cramped Victorian terraces swept away to make room for high-rise apartment blocks set in parkland. One has only to compare the

Ashby Institute to its neighbour on the site, the David Keir Building, to see the chasm of architectural thought that separates these two nearly contemporaneous buildings. Cruickshank and Seward brought to the design of the Ashby an informed knowledge and understanding of Modernism, to create a building of the highest quality.

DE

Our Lady of Bethlehem Abbey

PORTGLENONE   CO ANTRIM
PADRAIG MURRAY   1962–71

The building of an entire monastic complex in a modern idiom for any order is an unusual enough occurrence anywhere. As a rare instance for the Cistercians, Our Lady of Bethlehem Abbey at Portglenone, Co Antrim, may well be unique. It is also an impressive work of architecture.

Designed in 1960 by the young Dublin architect Padraig Murray, this large, three-storeyed and multi-gabled complex by the banks of the River Bann was built in the grounds of an 18th-century house in which monks from Mount Melleray Abbey in Co Waterford had established a monastery in 1948. The new building, started in 1962 and not finished until 1971, was originally intended to accommodate an anticipated community of over seventy monks, but numbers have never exceeded thirty.

Although uncompromisingly modern in style, it was, however, arranged in a traditional layout, with conjoined blocks grouped around a central landscaped cloister garth or open area. Initially designed and started before the findings of the Second Vatican Council on liturgical reform were made public, the original scheme underwent several changes in plan. As finally completed the accommodation comprised workshops, library, infirmary and sanitary facilities on the ground floor; refectory and kitchen, sacristy, offices, chapter house and abbey church on the first floor; and dormitories on the second floor. The latter were originally intended to be large open communal dormitories but were subsequently subdivided into separate cells in two of the wings, in the process lessening the effect of the vault-like ceilings.

The abbey church, which occupies the entire north side, with a seven-stage open-work concrete campanile to the east, dominates the view of the complex from the main public approach. It consists of a long, timber-roofed aisle-less nave lit by clerestory windows, with a high cage-like sanctuary from which projects a 'public church', or chapel, in a transeptal position, standing on pilotis and reached from below; this is arranged to overlook the high altar but not the monks' choir. The grand entrance gable at the west end of the main church, was, incidentally, originally orientated toward the site of an intended retreat house which was not built. Meanwhile, the main entrance to the entire building is set in the ground floor of the north elevation, and is by comparison very understated; it leads to a confessional

References

Girvan, W.D. and Rowan, A.J. *West Antrim.* Belfast: UAHS, 1970. 11, 24.

Larmour, P. Our Lady of Bethlehem Abbey. In Becker, A. Olley, J. and Wang, W. (eds). *20th century architecture: Ireland.* Munich & New York: Prestel Verlag, 1997. 128-129.

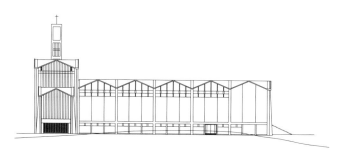

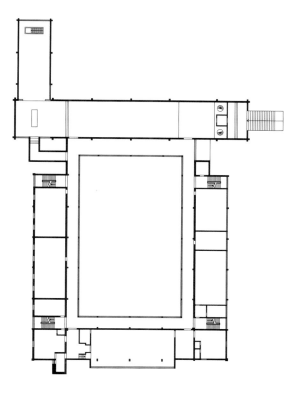

0 |———| 10

chapel on the ground floor which is open to the public.

Throughout the complex, construction is of reinforced concrete and grey concrete brick, with hyperbolic parabaloid timber shell roofs covered with copper. Unusually, the roofs are arranged in groups of four to each square bay so that they appear as a series of shallow gables along the eaves line. The architectural idiom of grid-like exposed frames with closely spaced mullions, containing brick infill panels and glazing which is mostly fixed directly into concrete frames, is used throughout, and the severely rectilinear character of the main elevations is softened only by the encroachment of ivy along the west elevation of the monastery. Whereas an overall coherence is given to the complex

by the use of a common roof structure for the disparate parts, the north wing is marked out as the church by the use of full-height battered buttresses, a rare but structurally necessary resort to the repertoire of traditional architectural forms.

The consistently rigorous approach to detailing that characterizes the exterior also extends to the interior. Here, finishes are also mainly plain, with some surfaces left as board-marked concrete. The only decorative effects are on floors, in the form of patterned parquet on landings, or pvc tiles in the cloisters where the monks stipulated coloured symbols such as the shamrock and St Brigid's cross. The lofty ceilinged church interior is particularly impressive, extremely long and narrow with an exceptionally wide altar of stone

which was also designed by Murray. An appropriately austere appearance is maintained throughout, reflecting the ethos of the Cistercian order.

Convent Chapel

COOKSTOWN   CO TYRONE
LAURENCE MCCONVILLE OF ROONEY & MCCONVILLE   1963–5

This Roman Catholic convent chapel is one of the gems of modern Irish church architecture, designed in 1963 by Laurence McConville of Rooney and McConville, architects of Belfast, and completed in 1965. Not only was it one of the most architecturally radical churches in Ireland in its time, being one of the first that was entirely modern in layout and design, but it was also one of the most successful integrations of the work of contemporary Irish ecclesiastical artists into a unified expression both inside and out.

The chapel is part of a two-storey extension to a late Victorian convent, and takes the form of a cubic first floor chapel raised on a recessed ground floor containing nine residential cells and a common room, all set at 45 degrees to the line of the front of the convent and attached by one corner to its former main entrance, thereby producing a bizarre juxtaposition of old and new. The reason for thus placing the extension on its diagonal axis was to allow light around both sides of it into rooms along the front of the convent building.

Whereas the ground floor cells are built of rubble sandstone cross-walls, the much larger upper-storey chapel is of concrete construction, of square plan, flat roofed, with pre-cast patterned concrete blocks to the exterior walls, decorated with a series of repetitive cross motifs. The two salient walls are blind but are animated by projecting bronze sculptural panels. These sculptures represent the four evangelists, on the south-east wall, and the 'Father', 'Son', and 'Holy Spirit', on the north-east wall, all designed and made by Patrick McElroy, the leading Irish art-metalworker at the time, who taught metalwork at the Dublin School of Art. It was presumably also McElroy who made the beaten copperwork panels for the door handles to the north boundary gateway outside, each depicting a saintly figure in primitive style.

References

Ireland's modern buildings. *Architects' Journal*, 144 (10), 1966. 634.

Oram, R.J. and Rankin, P.J. *Dungannon and Cookstown.* Belfast: UAHS,1971. 33.

Evans, D. *An introduction to modern Ulster architecture.* Belfast: UAHS, 1977. 55-56.

Rowan, A. J. *The buildings of Ireland: north west Ulster.* Harmondsworth: Penguin Books, 1979. 217.

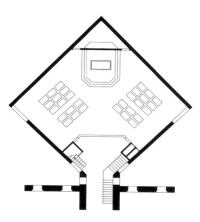
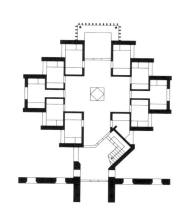

0 ————— 10

The interior of this textured concrete cubic block, entered at first floor level from the old convent, has a really intimate feel, derived in part from the small scale, but also due to the centralised arrangement of pews grouped around the altar, and an atmosphere of solemnity due to the arrangement of natural lighting by a roof lantern over the altar, while the satisfyingly plain finishes – Cumberland slate floor, rough-plastered walls, coffered structural timber roof, and chunky afrormosia pews – are complemented by an array of colourful and beautifully wrought contemporary artworks. These consist of two large stained glass windows by Patrick Pye of Dublin; the tabernacle, and a bronze crucifix on the wall behind the altar, both by Patrick McElroy; and enamelled copper stations of the cross, on the walls flanking the altar, by Benedict Tutty. The central focus of the interior, the altar itself, is boldly sculpted in stone by Michael Biggs, who presumably was also responsible for an accompanying lectern.

Elsewhere in the 1960s, the architect Laurence McConville went on to bring the work of Irish artists into a similar harmony with a modern church setting, at his extension to St MacNissi's Roman Catholic church at Magherahoney, Co Antrim, while his friend the architect Denis O'D Hanna similarly promoted local Ulster artists, as seen in the decoration and furnishing of two works for the Church of Ireland in Belfast, St Molua's, Stormont (1961-2), and the Church of the Pentecost at Cregagh (1961-3).

Ulster Museum Extension

BELFAST
FRANCIS PYM 1963–71

Time has done nothing to diminish the power and originality of this extraordinary building which first opened to the public in 1971; if anything the passing years have enhanced its standing as the major testament to high Modernism in the province and time has also made it increasingly unlikely that such an essay in reinforced concrete will be seen again. Construction costs for smooth shuttered concrete as a building finish have proved prohibitive and its use since the 1960s has been very limited, besides it does not weather well in our damp northern climate and it is liable to staining. Architects have tended to look to lightweight cladding as the outward expression of buildings; there

are great savings in time and money but the resulting architecture cannot claim the almost barbaric power of the great cubic projections and cantilevers of the Ulster Museum – it broods over the conifers of the Botanic Gardens like a mastodon.

Designed in 1963, as a competition-winning entry by Francis Pym, it is very much a child of its time. Robert Hughes, the distinguished art critic, has likened the appearance of art galleries and museums of that decade to fortresses or 'culture bunkers' which act as the keepers of a nation's treasures and keepers of its conscience. The National Theatre on the South Bank, London by Denys Lasdun

(1973) is a noted example of this tendency. (Although castigated by Prince Charles in the 1980s the building is currently regaining the respect that it deserves.) The Ulster Museum embodies a very wide range of cultural references in its design. Francis Pym has offered some revealing background information about his design approach in an interview with Paul O'Neill, an RIBA student, in 1985. He referred to his visit to Northern Ireland to study the site and to get a feel for the wider context and personality of the province. Dunluce Castle and its cliff top setting spoke to him as the isolated and embattled spirit of Ulster and there is in the Museum a sense of the introverted aggression of a

castle. The imagery of the fortress here metamorphoses into Cubism. This process, Pym has revealed, owes much to Mies van der Rohe's memorial to the Communist martyrs, Karl Liebknecht and Rosa Luxembourg. This monument in Berlin, which was destroyed by the Nazis, was a sculptural wall of brickwork with advancing and receding horizontal rectangular planes sporting a large star with an inscribed hammer and sickle. Pym has freely adapted this model into smooth steel-shuttered concrete losing nothing of the power of the original it seems in the translation. The façade has the geological grain of a quarry face, hewn and sculpted.

Other influences too are at work here but it is the spirit of Le Corbusier (l'esprit de Corb perhaps) that hangs over the design. The great French architect and apostle of Modernism was a potent force in architecture for much of the 20th century and some of his favourite themes and propositions are evident here; the strong cubic mass of the structure, the free plan, the interplay of interior volumes, the strip window and the roof gardens. There is even a reference to his pilotis beside the entrance. The corner of the building is raised clear of the ground to allow the space to flow under the building. (This area has since been enclosed to house the education centre.) The organisation of the

plan also acknowledges another Corbusian motif – the 'promenade' or route through the building establishing a particular emphasis. The Villa Savoie at Poissy (1927-31) is centred about a ramp which gradually reveals the interior spaces as it ascends to culminate at the roof terrace. Progress through the museum can also be seen as a ramp, or a series of ascending levels which bring the visitor to the top of the building and the prospect of the wider world. It is understood that this was how Pym saw his project, as a series of rising galleries starting with the local context and moving upwards through science and nature to end with the large art galleries at roof level. The progress however can be

read as a rectangular version of Frank Lloyd Wright's Guggenheim Museum New York (1956) in which the visitor rises by lift to the top level to begin a descent through the gallery which takes the form of a continuous spiral ramp. Pym's treatment of the staircase and lift which is strictly utilitarian in character would suggest its relative unimportance in the overall scheme. It should be noted however that the gradual rise (or descent) through the galleries comes at a price as it depends on numerous short flights of stairs which make the building a nightmare for wheelchair users and the subsequent fitting of chair lifts, to comply with current building regulations concerning

access, is a far from satisfactory solution to the problem.

In detail as well, the hand of Le Corbusier is evident, most dramatically perhaps in the great cantilevered entrance canopy which evokes the long loggia to the Assembly Buildings, Chandigarh, designed for the State Capitol of Punjab by Le Corbusier (1950-56). The window openings are punctuated by a staccato rhythm of heavy concrete mullions, which recalls the fenestration patterns of Corbusier's Monastery at La Tourette, Eveux, of 1956. The re-statement of façade features in the interior is another Corbusian motif, the long gliding lines of steps at the entrance,

with their echoes of neo-Classicism, reappear in the entrance foyer and rise to the low compressed space that leads to the machine hall. Here a pulpit-like balcony surveys the space at high level and re-states the high-sided open fronted balcony of the main façade which terminates the great Ionic entablature.

The original museum, a monumentally sculpted three-storied block of Portland stone, was designed by J.C. Wynnes, an Edinburgh architect, in 1911 and less than half the original stone was completed when work ceased in the late 20s. It belongs to the 'Wrenaissance' style (as Edwin Lutyens punningly calls it) that was a particular

favourite among architects for public and civic buildings in the early years of the 20th century. The City Hall and the Royal Courts of Justice, Belfast are local examples of the style that harks back to English architecture of the early 18th century and the work of Wren, Gibb and Hawskmoor. Typical of the style, Larmour has noted, is 'the massive often somewhat heavy effect associated with the use of stone in Renaissance architecture with a particular attention for rusticated masonry'.

Francis Pym's extension conforms to the general size and massing of the scheme as it was originally intended but in its fusion of the two worlds, of neo-Classicism and of

Corbusier, it is still stunning in its audacity. 'The solution of splicing the two together' as Robert McKinstry has written, 'so that as your eye travels from right to left, a transformation scene takes place that is daring, witty and disturbing, but it succeeds'. The assessors for the design competition showed judgement and strong nerves in selecting this scheme as the winner.

The extension enclosed the unfinished courtyard of the old museum. This space has since been given a translucent roof and has the feel of a court in a Renaissance palazzo. It now houses the dinosaur exhibition. The new machine hall flanks

this space, a large cavernous volume dedicated to local industry with a massive coffered roof in concrete. These two major elements which rise through the building are the heart of the scheme; the galleries are wrapped around them.

The design of this building predates the publication of Robert Venturi's *Complexity or contradiction in architecture* by three years. This seminal work is generally held to have ushered in a new wave of architectural thought; Venturi declared that 'less is a bore' and called for more meaning and for 'messy vitality' in design. His professed admiration for the playfulness of Edwin Lutyens and for the

quirky and the strange in Mannerist architecture of the Renaissance was a force for change that introduced a concern for context and anticipated the rise of Postmodernism. This building contains an impressive range of diverse and erudite references, as noted, and a delight in the unexpected. The mysterious and dark unfolding of its interior spatial sequences is a world away from the orthodoxies of its time. Robert Venturi's own extension of a classical building, the Sainsbury wing of the National Gallery London is, in comparison, a very timid response. The façade of the new wing, facing Trafalgar Square, adopts the classical vocabulary of the existing building at its closest point

and gradually assumes a more neutral expression as it moves away. Francis Pym's solution, some twenty five years earlier, is the robust integration of old and new and he interlocks the Cubist massing of the new galleries with the unfinished neo-Classical building by extending its rusticated ashlar walling. The new galleries are the outward expression of the interior volumes and their increase in scale as the building rises resembles the uncoiling of a giant spring.

The entire project has taken on the status of folklore and has something of the Sydney Opera House saga about it. An unknown architect wins a major international competition but resigns from the project

before it is completed. In this case, the Department of Finance NI who had commissioned the building took over the supervision of the contract. A member of Pym's London staff, Paddy Lawson of Portaferry who had worked on the competition, joined the Architect's Branch of the Department of Finance to maintain continuity in the implementation of the design. Another Ulsterman, Brian Lowe, was responsible for the interiors – in effect there was a considerable local input. Francis Pym who never saw his work completed turned to the church and became an Anglican chaplain in London – this building was his only major project. The launch could not have come at a worse

References

McKinstry, R. Contemporary architecture. In Longley, M. (ed). *Causeway: the arts in Ulster*. Belfast: The Arts Council of Northern Ireland, 1971. 27-37.

Mr Pym passes by. *Building Design*, (63), 1971. 10-11.

Larmour, P. The inter-war years in Belfast. *Big A3* (The Magazine of the Department of Architecture, QUB, Belfast), 1973. Unpaginated.

Leitch, C. *A building of galleries: a study of the growth of the Ulster Museum.* Queen's University, Belfast School of Architecture dissertation, 1994.

Clarke, P. Belfast's upward spiral. *Perspective*, 13 (3), 2004. 72-75.

time; in 1971 Belfast was at the worst of the Troubles and although times have greatly improved since then the building has never been accorded the status it merits. In 2004 a Scottish architect, Paul Clarke, hailed it as 'a building of major architectural importance. It awaits a wider discovery in the world of international tourism.' The passing years have not been kind, the chronic lack of funding, the growing pressure on exhibition and storage space (although the roof terraces and balconies have remained 'out of bounds' to the public) and the need for car parking have cluttered the delightfully undulating concrete approach to the building. 'Now is the time' as Clarke has suggested, with

'the energy and confidence that is taking shape in Belfast to restore, clean and upgrade the shell and perhaps introduce new buildings into the Botanic Gardens to intensify the experience of the area as a major Cultural/Museum Park'. The idea of linking the museum with the forecourt of the Lanyon Building, Queen's University, could widen and add to that experience.

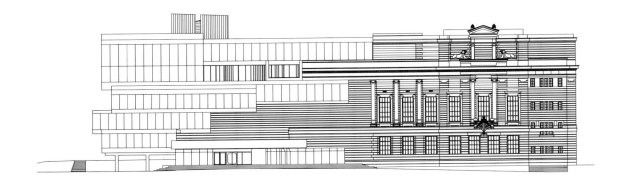

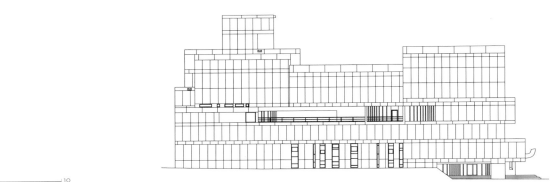

0 ⌐_____⌐ 10

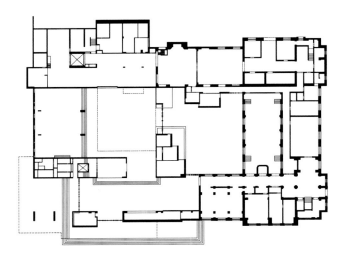

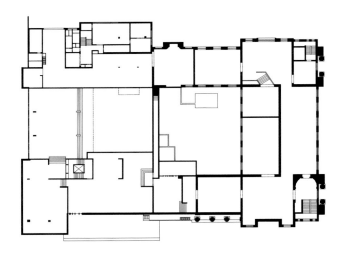

0 ⌐___⌐ 10

GROUND FLOOR

UPPER GROUND FLOOR

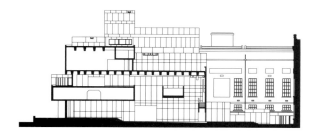

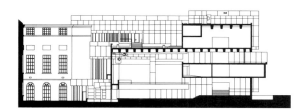

0 _____ 10

SECOND FLOOR

Antrim County Hall

BALLYMENA   CO ANTRIM
BURMAN GOODALL & PARTNERS   1964–71

'Without doubt the finest complete modern building in Northern Ireland' was the comment in the *Architects' Journal* when County Hall opened in 1971. It is an almost exact contemporary of another contender for high architectural honours – the Ulster Museum extension, Belfast; both buildings were the outcome of international competitions and both brought to light, for the first time, the talents of young English designers. County Hall received an RIBA Award in 1971 as did the Ulster Museum in the following year but each building, though a major architectural event, has a markedly different personality. This building draws some of its inspiration

from the non-dogmatic Modernism of the Finnish master Alvar Aalto but other references come into play.

The decision to move Antrim County Council from Belfast to near the geographic heart of the county at Ballymena, was taken in the early 1960s when the splendid site of 9 hectares, on the Galgorm estate, came available. The building programme called for administrative offices, a council chamber and an assembly hall seating 700. The site is fringed with mature trees and slopes gently from east to west; the new building occupies centre stage and is linked to a small copse of deciduous trees.

The five-storey offices in red brick are strung along the contours running north-south and the detached assembly hall and council chamber look out over the falling ground to the west.

The presence of a large red brick building may seem somewhat incongruous in rural parkland but the young English architects 'never thought of any other material' when they entered the competition. The tradition of brick built country houses is strong in England but to Irish eyes the use of render and stonework is more sympathetic. However the linen mills of the 19th century, multi-storied brick structures, often stood

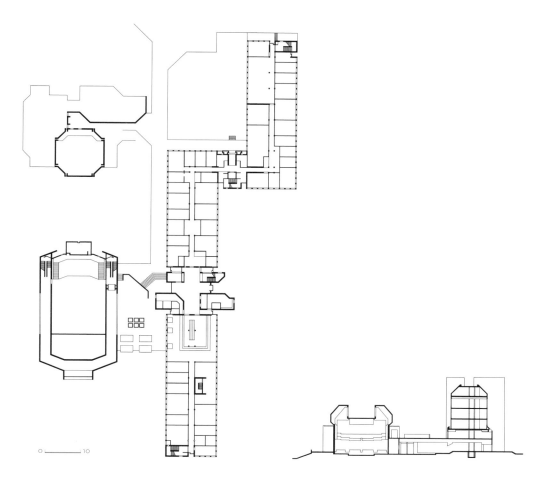

in open country and as a familiar part of our industrial heritage made for a relevant precedent. The architects were interested in reworking the imagery of this Victorian legacy. The effect is undeniably startling and dramatic: the assessors for the competition praised the scheme for its 'siting, scale and choice of materials'.

The office range is fragmented into three parts to reduce the scale, two vertical cores intercepting the long north south progression. The entrance core presents blank towering planes to the visitor and in the other, twin flues soar high above the raised roof level of the core, like factory

chimneys. The sheer sense of the monumental however recalls Louis Kahn's Richards Laboratories, University of Pennsylvania (1957-61), where the external expression of the vertical ducts has given rise to the nickname 'ducthenge'.

The architects referred to an 'Aalto-like feeling' created by brick walling surrounded by trees as a source of inspiration. There are other associations here with the Finn whose work brought to Modernism the use of traditional materials such as brick, slate, copper and timber, often in an innovative manner and whose organic approach made for architecture of humanity

with symbolic overtones. Here the long horizontal banding of the windows and the warm red-brown brickwork recalls the façades of Aalto's National Pensions Institute, Helsinki (1952-56) in particular. This composition of three- and four-storey blocks frames a sequence of outdoor spaces or 'piazzas' through which people pass as they approach the building so that in Aalto's words the 'organic movement of people' is 'incorporated in the shaping of the site' and the path through the complex is given special emphasis and is 'treated like a rite of passage'. (It means too that the external spaces associated with a building take on an active human

use rather than being consigned to merely decorative site treatments.) An event of this kind is the progression from Galgorm Road towards the public entrance: it begins with the end view of the two office blocks, separated by twin flues, then continues along the rising brick paved concourse to the ramparted podium to the offices, which rise to one side and the free standing council chamber and assembly hall on the other. The journey ends at the emphatic walls of brickwork which announce the partially concealed and surprisingly modest entrance.

The council chamber and assembly hall rise above podium level like Baroque chapels. The octagonal council chamber, where fragmented brick walling clusters about a fragmented pyramid, has a complexity of form as 'diverting as any modern sculpture'. The roof lights rise up like pram hoods and their canted angles clad in slate are also used to spectacular effect on the assembly hall. An antecedent to this form is the Elephant House at London Zoo of 1964 by Casson Condor and Partners where fortress like walls are topped with canted roof lights, clad in copper – 'sky scuttles' as Casson calls them.

The assembly hall is a multi-purpose auditorium with a deep balcony, a level floor and a raised stage at one end; it functions particularly well as a concert hall as the acoustic is good. In a building of many incidents the staff dining room is a memorable space; it looks out to the landscape to the west over the sunken walkway which leads to the council chamber.

Since its enthusiastic reception in 1971, County Hall has come in for some criticism and has had its share of problems although it is still being used for its original purpose today. The glazing to the offices has been replaced and the building now stands as testament to the originality and sense of bravura of two young designers from

References

McKinstry, R. Building study: County Hall. *Architects' Journal*, 154(47), 1971. 1169-1183.

Frampton, K. *Modern architecture: a critical history*. London : Thames & Hudson, 1980.

Casson, H. *Hugh Casson's London*. London : J.M. Dent & Sons Ltd, 1983.

England. Both were working as architectural assistants in a Birmingham office when they entered the competition in 1964. They set up in practice together and Anthony Goodall moved to Ballymena to become site architect. (It is sad to recall that Tony Burman, his partner, was killed in a car crash in 1971 and did not see the opening of the building.) A generation later another Birmingham firm, Glenn Howells Architects, won an international competition for the design of the Armagh Theatre and maintained the process of bringing distinction to, and enriching, Ulster architecture.

St Aengus's Church

BURT   CO DONEGAL
LIAM MCCORMICK OF CORR & MCCORMICK   1965–7

The name that stands out as the central figure in the development of modern church architecture, not just in Ulster but in Ireland as a whole, is that of Liam McCormick. Over a period of four decades this gifted architect was responsible for an impressive series of outstanding churches, all but one of them designed for the Roman Catholic denomination. Many of them were built in his own home county of Donegal, including his most famous example, the RIAI Gold Medal-winning Church of St Aengus at Burt which was to bring him unprecedented acclaim and lead to his eventual international reputation.

This rural church stands on an open hillside overlooking Lough Swilly, its sculpturally treated asymmetrical form integrating perfectly with the mountainous setting. A combination of new directives on Catholic liturgy and McCormick's romantic response to the presence of an ancient circular stone-walled fort, Grianan of Aileach, on a hilltop above the site, provided the inspiration for the design. Here he abandoned the traditional rectangular or basilican plan of his previous churches and produced a circular plan, something that was a really new and original concept in Irish church architecture at the time.

The plan is formed by two circles, one placed tangentially within the other, the crescent of space between the walls being used to house the baptistery and subsidiary offices, so that the church appears circular both inside and outside. It is built with a barrel-like squared rubble stone exterior wall, the inner one being concrete blocks with a plaster finish, with a plastered steel and timber ceiling supported on an inner ring of steel columns. Above a continuous glass clerestory, on the outside, the tent-like copper roofing with up-turned overhang sweeps up eccentrically to form a conical spire which contains a lantern light placed directly over the altar.

The circular theme is all-pervasive. Surrounding the base of the church outside is a moat with four small circular pools formed of granite cobbles, recovered

References

Roman Catholic Church, Burt, Co Donegal. *Architectural Review*, 143(855),1968. 361-2.

Rowan, A. J. *The buildings of Ireland: north west Ulster.* Harmondsworth: Penguin Books, 1979. 157-158.

Larmour, P. Church of St Aengus. In Becker, A. Olley, J. Wang, W. (eds). *20th century architecture: Ireland.* Munich and New York: Prestel, 1997. 131.

Larmour, P. My pagan building: Liam McCormick's church at Burt. *Irish Architectural Review*, 2, 2000. 14-24.

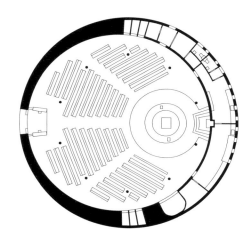 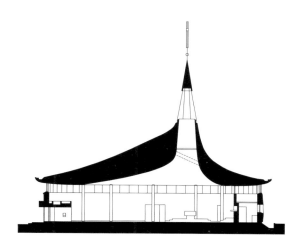

from the old quayside in Derry, whilst the brown brick path leading up to the church is laid in circular patterns.

Inside the church the curvilinear theme is sustained by the shallow steps that encircle the altar, and by the seating. The steel columns supporting the roof are also circular as is their formation, although the ring they comprise is placed concentrically within the circle of the exterior rather than the interior wall, which produces an appropriate effect of optical movement toward the off-centre sanctuary. Apart from this rather Baroque-like spatial play inside, the treatment of the interior is very plain, with white-painted surfaces to walls and ceiling.

The work of various artists provides a foil to the plainness of the interior surfaces, however, and indeed forms a very distinctive and pleasing feature of the building. It includes stained glass by Helen Moloney; the crucifix, altar and font by Imogen Stuart; the enamelled tabernacle by Patrick McElroy; and candlesticks by Brendan Friel. The woven hanging on the ambo or lectern was by Veronica Rowe, while the vestments were designed by Helen Moloney. The most intriguing artwork is outside the building where a sculptured free-standing wall in cast concrete by Oisin Kelly depicts the history of the site with reference to both St Aengus and to Grianan fort. One of Kelly's symbols on the wall, a maze pattern

with a cross, was also used for the circular handles to the great beaten copper entrance doors of the church and elsewhere inside. All these associated artworks were skilfully co-ordinated by the architect in a very successful scheme which was conceived and executed with sensitivity, imagination, and skill.

St Aengus's church was awarded the RIAI Triennial Gold Medal in 1971 for buildings erected in the years 1965-7.

Victoria College

BELFAST
SHANKS & LEIGHTON   1968–72

Victoria College is magnificently sited in the demesne of Drumglass House, a Victorian mansion in the Italianate style which now acts as the centrepiece of the new buildings. The house, currently the College's boarding department, occupies the crown of the site and the ground in front falls steeply towards Cranmore Park to the south. The buildings are framed by cedars of Lebanon, oak, ash, beech and conifers – a handsome legacy of planting which adds to the architectural experience. The two major items of accommodation are strongly contrasted in expression; the classroom wing is lofty and columnar and the assembly hall monolithic and introverted: both can be interpreted as conversations with Le Corbusier.

The classrooms are strung along the contours at the edge of the escarpment in three storeys; free standing columns in smooth precast concrete rise through two floors to carry the oversailing top floor which takes on the role of the entablature of the classical orders and binds the composition together. The heavy form of the top floor in dark exposed-aggregate concrete, supported on elongated columns, refers more to the repertoire of Le Corbusier at the Monastery of La Tourette, Lyons (1957) than to classical precedent. The board-marked concrete used on the gable walls is another Corbusian feature and the overall grouping and massing of the project echoes his Pavillon Suisse, Cité Universitaire, Paris (1930-32).

There, the four-storied hostel accommodation forms a severely rectangular block which is juxtaposed with the free-flowing, single-storied spaces which house the communal areas. At Victoria College, the architects have developed this theme by introducing an imaginative play of levels, occasioned by the sloping site, and by the use of the dining hall to link the classrooms to the old house and to frame the entrance area.

A glazed lobby connects the classrooms with the free-standing assembly hall (and music department), an emphatic presence in board-marked concrete with a shaped and faceted roof structure finished in sheet metal. The hall, which is superimposed

upon the gymnasium below, is massively cantilevered on three sides to form an external balcony. The interior exposes heavy cranked roof-beams, their mass and board-marked finish recalls Corbusier's work at Chandigarh and the rustic brick walling and timber finishes are rich and sombre in tone.

The gymnasium and changing rooms are cut into the slope of the site and externally the reinforced concrete retaining walls are given a vertical ribbed profile with jagged edges which expose the aggregate. (A technique favoured by the English architect Hugh Casson and used at his Microbiology Centre, Royal Victoria Hospital, Belfast – he referred to it as 'bashed' concrete.)

The sixth form centre, which likewise required some excavation, is situated at the east end of the classrooms from where a staircase descends to an open space overlooking a small courtyard. The suite of study rooms is arranged about this space and a lecture room raises its raked floor in a jutting cantilever in ribbed concrete.

Drumglass House is flanked to the west by the preparatory school, a concrete cluster of chunky octagonal classrooms with tall pointed roof lights, like witches' hats in a pantomime. On the west side the lightest of glazed links houses the dining room and connects the school and the old house. The courtyard to the rear contains the new school library, a later addition.

The quality of the external spaces, framed by buildings and linked by the circulation routes which provide a narrative thread, is important. The College entrance from Cranmore Park leads to a winding path which weaves its way through stands of conifers towards the tall columnar façade of the teaching wing. It passes the cantilevered gallery of the assembly hall (its underside a waffle slab), which casts a deep shadow, and arrives at a level concourse partially cut into the hillside where the ribbed retaining wall projects a bastion-like staircase to the classrooms. The pupils' route proceeds behind and below the assembly hall in a semi-subterranean passage which overlooks the gymnasium and culminates in a flight

Victoria College

of steps which leads to the main entrance forecourt in front of Drumglass House. From there the glazed dining hall affords through-glimpses of the open court at the rear of the classroom wing.

The architecture seems to belong to the high summer of Modernism when the use of concrete found expressive and sculptural form and suggested that its high ideals were about to be realized. The use of exposed concrete, however, had inherent technical problems even when handled with the finesse and attention to detail shown by these architects. Even here some remedial work has been required to the exterior finish and a painting scheme has

been carried out. It cannot be claimed that the architecture has suffered materially although some of the definition of the board-marking has been forfeited.

The College received a Concrete Society Award in 1973 and an RIBA Commendation in the same year.

References

Concrete Society 1973 award (Certificate of Commendation): Victoria College, Belfast. *Irish Builder & Engineer*, 1974. 122.

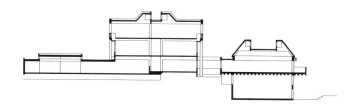

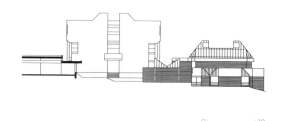

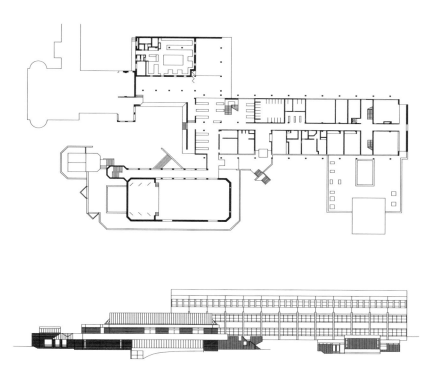

St Michael's Church

CREESLOUGH   CO DONEGAL
LIAM MCCORMICK OF LIAM MCCORMICK & PARTNERS   1970–1

One of the most visually satisfying of modern Irish churches, St Michael's is notable for its response to the landscape, providing a perfect illustration of its architect's respect for the place of nature in design. It stands on a ridge outside the village of Creeslough in a landscape dominated by Muckish Mountain whose distinctive profile in the distance is echoed in the outline of the church.

The building is outstanding for its plastic treatment of white roughcast walls which follow the curves of the fan-shaped plan. To the front these walls present a strong, battered, almost solid face, the roof being suppressed, with very small windows and a deep set entrance to the main road. Away from the road, however, a carefully positioned broad full height window (originally a simple three-light arrangement) in the sweep of the rear wall allows a view over rough pastures to the mountain beyond, a constant reminder of the inspiration for the profile of the building.

Nicely balancing the building mass on the entrance front are a free-standing cross and a detached openwork steel-framed belfry, while between them on the stone-paved terrace against the wall of the church lies a circular pool designed to collect rainwater channelled off the roof by means of a concrete trough to run down a heavy spiked chain into the pool.

The influence of Le Corbusier's much-publicised pilgrimage chapel at Ronchamp of the early to mid-1950s is evident not only in the curving profile and battered overall sculptural form of the church but also in the random arrangement of deep-set windows in the area of wall between the pool and the main entrance.

The immensely thick walls actually comprise two skins, the outer one battered and the inner one vertical. Diaphragm walls connect

References

Wright, L. Donegal fan: Church at Creeslough, Co Donegal, Ireland. *Architectural Review*, 151(901),1972. 180-184.

Larmour, P. In the name of the father. *Perspective*, 5 (2), 1996. 30-43.

Larmour, P. St Michael's Church. In Becker, A. Olley, J. and Wang, W. (eds.) *20th century architecture: Ireland*. Munich and New York: Prestel, 1997. 139.

the two skins at intervals and in the deep cavity thus formed are placed the steel columns that support the roof trusses. Also ingeniously housed in the space between the two walls are a sacrament chapel and a baptistery at the front, both with curved ends inside, while along the rear curving wall are confessionals and sacristies. A curvilinear theme is present elsewhere inside: curved pews with curved lighting units above them focus attention on the rectangular altar that stands on two circular platforms and is lit by a circular roof light.

In an interior otherwise characterised by a rural simplicity, stained glass in the chapel and various altar furnishings add effective notes of brilliant colour, while originally the clever use of flowing water served a symbolic function in the baptistery. Helen Moloney designed and made the stained glass and also designed an altar tapestry which was worked by Veronica Rowe, while John Behan provided the tabernacle enamels, and Ruth Brandt was responsible for the lettering on the glazed doorscreen.

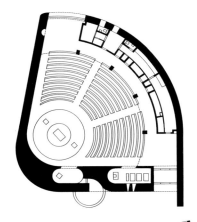

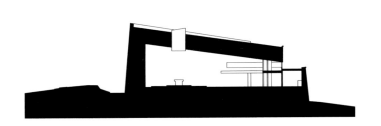

0 ———————— 10

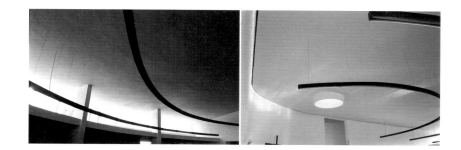

Castle Building, Stormont

BELFAST
DAVE RODGERS & STAN BLAYNEY OF THE ARCHITECTS' BRANCH, DEPARTMENT OF FINANCE   1970–7

As it stands today the building is only a part of a larger project which was never realized; only five of the nine towers and associated offices projected were built. It belongs to the 'megastructure' form which was an obsession among architects and planners of the 50s and 60s and is now considered something of an architectural dinosaur. In its heyday 'city centres, universities and housing schemes were being proposed in megastructure form' all around the world, as Reyner Banham commented, and 'visionary megamovements like the Japanese Metabolists and the British Archigram group threatened to monopolise the magazines'. Size alone does not make a megastructure although

they are all large buildings. Banham defines a megastructure as a structure that is made up of modular units and capable of great or even unlimited expansion. It is also a structural framework onto which units can be built, or 'plugged in' or 'clipped on'.

Castle Building follows the megastructure form as it is undeniably large and uses modular units. The structural framework consists of five towers, or cores, built in brickwork. These house the essential services, stairs, lifts, toilets and air handling. They rise as dark faceted towers above the five identical and horizontally stratified office blocks which are 'plugged' into them. The layout of the scheme can

be read as a chequerboard in which the black squares, for instance, represented the office accommodation and the white squares the courtyard spaces between them; the cores are situated at the points where the squares meet. The originality of this format is that it is indeed capable of infinite extension in any direction and it can easily adapt to changes in level as it does here.

The pavilion-like four-storey offices are square in plan, with four identical façades. Their framed structure uses in situ waffle slab floors with exposed soffits and exposed-aggregate precast concrete panels to the exterior. The first, second and third

References

Banham, R. *Megastructure: urban futures of the recent past.* London: Thames and Hudson, 1976. 8 and dust jacket.

SITE PLAN   0 ⌞_____⌟ 50000

TYPICAL ELEVATION

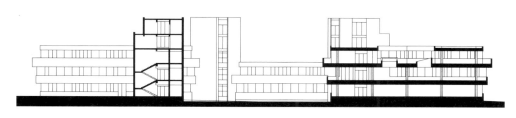

SECTIONAL ELEVATION   0 ⌞_____⌟ 10

floors project progressively to cut down solar glare and top floor offices are set back to accommodate the air-input ducting which runs peripherally behind the deep parapet. At this level the suite of offices is laid out in a central square courtyard which allows roof lighting to penetrate the deep plan of the offices below. This floor was raised – an early response to designing for the new technology. When the building opened, free-standing columns formed an arcade to the double height dining room and mezzanine lounge of the office block which flanks the entrance. It added spatial play and incident, but time has brought changes and this feature has now disappeared and the columns are

enclosed by a glazed wall. The rearmost block of the five was taken over by the Northern Ireland Office in the mid-1990s, prior to the Belfast Agreement talks, and some modifications were necessary. Other changes too mean that some of the 'grand' vision of the project has been lost. Seen from the Newtownards Road nearby it retains its strong visual appeal; snugly sited among gently rolling woodlands, its towers, linked by the deep shadow lines of the offices, provide companion pieces to Stormont Castle which rises behind.

The University of Ulster at Jordanstown, by Building Design Partnership (completed 1970), is another local example of the

megastructure; it employs a horizontal and linear structure of circulation and services and the teaching blocks which are 'clipped' onto it, extend at right angles to it on both sides. It lacks, however, the 'modular' discipline and strict format of the Stormont example and the capacity of extension in all directions.

DE

Portadown New Technical College

CRAIGAVON   CO ARMAGH
SHANKS LEIGHTON KENNEDY FITZGERALD   1972–6

The firm Shanks Leighton Kennedy FitzGerald started with the partnership formed by Donald Shanks and Edwin Leighton in 1960. They were then joined by Jim Kennedy in 1964, followed in 1965 by Joe FitzGerald, both arrivals from Scotland. To the expertise in schools building already within the firm in the person of Donald Shanks, who had been Belfast Education Architect from 1954 to 1960, Kennedy and FitzGerald brought to the practice a particularly vigorous approach to design – born of a deep admiration for the structural forms and beton-brut finishes of late Le Corbusier – which saw the larger partnership forge a robust and boldly expressive style largely through a series of educational buildings. These included

Reilly's Cross School in Co Fermanagh (1966-70), Enniskillen Collegiate School for Girls (1967), Victoria College extension, Belfast (1968-72) and Enniskillen Model School (1973-75), all strongly modelled in form, but the most imposing, monumental, and aggressively shaped was Portadown New Technical College.

Built in an area of Craigavon, on the outskirts of Portadown, this impressive and uncompromisingly modern structure is a tour-de-force in concrete and glass that imposes a strong but somewhat alien form on its gently sloping site. A multi-level complex, it consists of a number of separate and clearly defined blocks – high school, technical college, sports hall,

workshops, and heat engines – placed at various levels to suit the contours of the site but linked to each other by underground and overhead corridors. Off to one side stands a detached boiler house block.

The general construction of all the blocks is reinforced concrete with supplementary steelwork being employed for some of the large-span roofs, as in the large workshop, sports hall, and central assembly hall. Externally the buildings are finished in board-marked in situ concrete, handled with exemplary skill, with evident care in the arranging of patterns. These are mostly alternate horizontally and vertically marked half-storey-height stratified bands but also include more decoratively arranged

References

Evans, D. *An introduction to modern Ulster architecture.* Belfast: UAHS, 1977. 37-38.

Larmour, P. Technical College, Portadown. In Becker, A. Olley, J. Wang, W. (eds). *20th century architecture: Ireland.* Munich and New York: Prestel, 1997. 144-145.

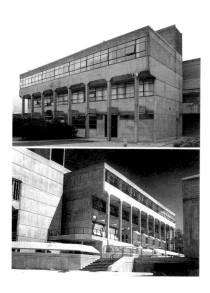

diagonal shapes on the boiler house block. There are also some areas of exposed aggregate in the robustly ribbed walls around the concourse, while exposed concrete coffer-moulded undersides to overhead linking corridors and some oversailing bays add to the range of textures outside. Similar coffers also appear inside, where finishes are mainly fair-faced brickwork and board-marked concrete to walls. Unfortunately many of these exposed concrete surfaces have been painted over in recent years thus spoiling the visual cohesion of the group of blocks and the delicacy of detail in the board-markings.

The central focus of the entire complex is the Technical College block where a large internal assembly hall forms the core with classrooms, laboratories, library and administration offices grouped all around at five different levels. Whilst the whole complex is characterised by highly modelled shapes, with deep recesses and angled planes, this central block is the most boldly treated, with towering cantilevered masses of fortress-like solidity on the entrance front, containing recessed bands of windows which have irregularly spaced mullions derived from Le Corbusier's monastery of La Tourette. Along the sides, oversailing top floors are hoisted on tall thin columnar piers through which canted bays in purple brick and projecting square oriels give expression to various rooms.

Throughout the complex, elements shift and align in new relationships as one moves around the hewn and angled forms; the landscaped pedestrian walkways and courtyards between the various blocks adding to the spatial quality which, combined with a formal inventiveness, is one of the chief merits of the building. As a highly complex but well controlled design that shows a mastery of sculptural form, it is surely one of the most significant buildings of its era never to have won an architectural award even if the use of virtually monolithic concrete has subsequently proved to be problematic.

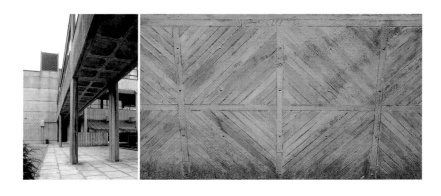

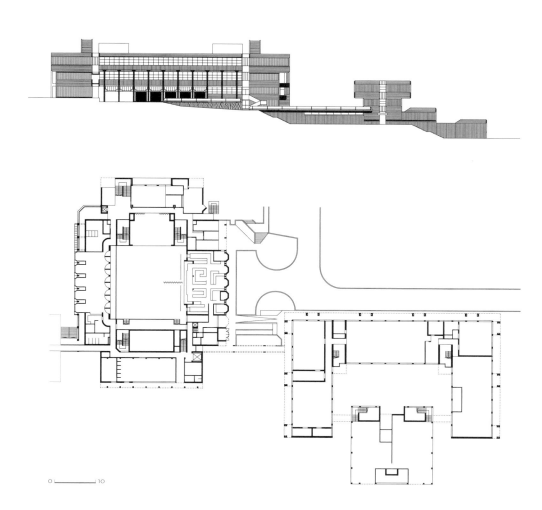

St Conal's Church

GLENTIES   CO DONEGAL
LIAM MCCORMICK OF LIAM MCCORMICK & PARTNERS   1974–6

At St Conal's church in Glenties, Liam McCormick broke from the curving forms of his churches at Burt and Creeslough and returned to a more traditional layout with a rectilinear plan, but in a very original shape.

The church is a boldly formed A-frame type, its high steeply pitched and slated roof sweeping down almost to ground level, with tall gable ends of white roughcast. Typically the architect has wedded the building to the landscape, placing it well back from the road and set deeply into the sloping site, with landscaped grounds in front and mature trees retained as a backdrop behind. Asbestos slates cover the roof which consists of two unequal

pitches, the slope to the rear stopping short of the main ridge height to allow a long strip of clerestory glazing. Along the base of the roof, at a low eaves level, a recessed glazed wall runs the entire length of the front, broken at regular intervals by the buttress-like piers which support the roof. Here rainwater is collected in a massive lead-lined gutter and disgorged by cast metal animal-head waterspouts into a transverse ornamental pool along the length of the building. These gargoyles which depict animals native to the area – sheep, goats and cattle – were designed by the Irish sculptor Imogen Stuart. Lead panelled doors, also by Stuart, decorated with an owl, a cockerel, a

tortoise, a hedgehog, a dove and a snail, as well as the liturgical symbol of the fish, form the main entrance which is reached by a footpath crossing over the pool.

The interior is as dramatic as the exterior is bold, the narrow entrance opening up to reveal a small day chapel to the left, through a glazed screen which was a later addition, with the much larger main church to the right. To reduce excavation into the steeply sloping hillside, which included a long shelf of natural rock, a split floor level was created within the main church interior, which adds to the spatial interest created by unequal roof pitches. The gable wall behind the altar was also provided with

References

Evans, D. *An introduction to modern Ulster architecture.* Belfast: UAHS, 1977. 61-62.

2 Ulster churches. *Architectural Review,* 143 (973), 1978. 171-174.

St Conal's Church, Glenties. *Irish Builder & Engineer,* 121 (5), 1979. 44.

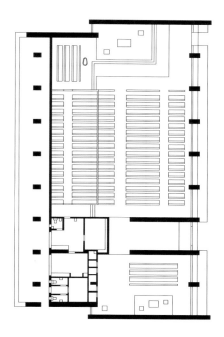
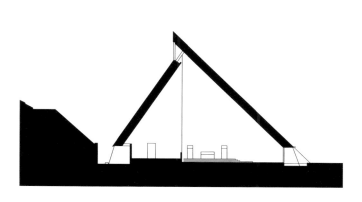

a stagger, at the change in floor level, and a full height slit window inserted to illuminate the sanctuary. Natural lighting otherwise comes from the high clerestory strip and from the low level windows that overlook the ornamental pool and herb garden.

The use of plain and simple materials including concrete slab flooring, white plastered walls and rough boarded ceilings, accentuates the geometric shapes that dominate this dramatic interior, while a range of impressive artworks and furnishings provide more localised interest. These include a boldly formed altar and ambo in Liscannor slabs from Co Clare, sculpted by Michael Biggs; a

stone high cross in the sanctuary sculpted by Imogen Stuart; and stations of the cross modelled by Nell Murphy, who was also responsible for the three large wall-mounted figures, representing St Conal, Our Lady, and St Columcille, in the entrance lobby at the rear of the nave, executed in sculpted and painted plaster. Elsewhere, Ruth Brandt executed a lettered plaque, while Joy McCormick, wife of the architect, created a set of vestments.

Despite its large size the church is not obtrusive, a result not only of McCormick's skilful siting but also of the sensitive landscaping, designed originally by Florence Woods, in harmony with the

surrounding trees, all of which helps to soften the bold angular forms and provides a foil to the tall Japanese-inspired entrance gateway of metal girders set up at the roadside approach in front of the church.

St Conal's gained a commendation from the RIAI in its Triennial Gold Medal Award for 1974-76.

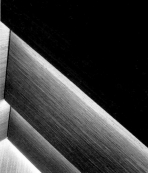

Our Lady of Lourdes Church

STEELSTOWN   CO LONDONDERRY
LIAM MCCORMICK OF LIAM MCCORMICK & PARTNERS   1975–6

The budget for this building, located in what was a new housing area outside Londonderry, and part of a wider church building programme then underway, was severely limited, but despite the priorities of low cost and speedy building, McCormick met the challenge of providing a building of the scale, and of the appearance of permanence appropriate for a church, with a memorable conception.

In plan-form and general appearance this church at Steelstown is similar to McCormick's work at Glenties. Externally very angular it consists of a simple steel structure with a steeply pitched roof that almost touches the ground, stepped back in three successive planes, clad with blue asbestos slates, with long narrow slit windows (originally of corrugated plastic sheeting) at the changes of roof levels, extending almost full-height. No gutters are used and so the rain can cascade down the roofs into an ornamental pool which lies at the base of the buttress-like piers outside the low level windows across the front, similar to that at Glenties. Unlike Glenties, however, the gables are of timber framing, sheeted in boarding and hung with asbestos slates, instead of being built of traditional masonry walling, and the main entrance is housed in a porch of triangular form projecting at the west end.

Inside, there is a strong west-to-east processional axis, but although the three-stage roof outside might suggest the conventional divisions of nave, choir, and chancel, this is not a traditionally ordered space. A weekday chapel, enclosed by glazing, lies to one side and looks on to the main space which is dominated by a great tent-like roof of rough-sawn hemlock boarding. Most of the natural lighting is concealed, and comes from the

References

2 Ulster churches. *Architectural Review*, 143 (973), 1978. 171-174.

Cooper, M. Large church on a small budget. *Building Design*, (413), 1978. 20-21

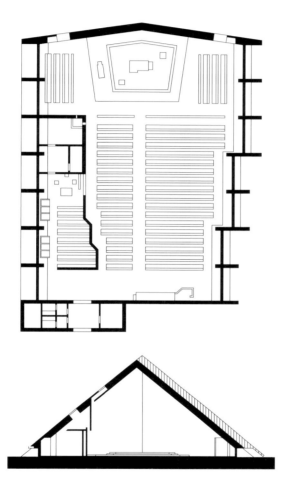

0 ⌞_____⌟ 10

tall recessed roof lights, the windows low down at the sides providing little more than a constricted but tantalising view of the pools and pebbles outside, rather than adding much to the illumination inside. The overall effect of this open and lofty main interior space is very impressive. Each end wall is marked by a great triangular gable, the one at the west relieved by an organ case of correspondingly angled shape, while the one at the east contains a visual focus in the life-size crucifix that dominates the stepped sanctuary podium. As usual, the church was enhanced by a team of McCormick's favourite artists. The

crucifix was the work of Helen Moloney who also created the symbols on the altar and ambo. The enamelled metalwork in the weekday chapel and elsewhere was by Patrick McElroy, the stations of the cross were by Sister Aloysius, and the sculptured group of 'Our Lady of Lourdes' was carved in wood by Oisin Kelly.

Outside, the setting of this dramatic and evocative church was completed by some Japanese-inspired touches that suit the temple-like form of the building, such as the simple landscaping scheme of trees and a loose boulder rockery, but in particular,

the steel-girder gateway and its cross. Steelstown church gained a commendation from the RIBA in 1978.

Dungannon District Council Offices

DUNGANNON   CO TYRONE
SHANKS LEIGHTON KENNEDY FITZGERALD   1976–80

This compact and prismatic study in red brickwork is ordered by a strict geometric discipline which sets up a sequence of striking and sometimes spectacular architectural events. The use of a system of numbers, ratios, axes, grids or even a more arcane agenda, to control the design of a building is as old as architecture itself and to some it is synonymous with it. That buildings should pertain to some abstract or higher discipline than the demands of programme has been an enduring fascination among architects. Here the controlling geometry for the building springs from the topography and layout of the site on the edge of this hilltop town. Circular Road forms the eastern boundary

of the site and it cuts across the contours of the falling ground at about 45°. The premise that the office accommodation should run parallel with the contour lines and that the main entrance and council chamber should face the entrance on Circular Road set up the diagonal emphasis which gives the design such vibrancy.

The Council Offices building is sited halfway down the site and the approach road winds past trees and small car parking spaces indented into the hill before arriving at the forecourt of this unpretentious but engaging building. Its footprint resembles a large square from which large sections have been subtracted to leave angular and

geometric forms. The building diminishes in width as it descends and the stepped form of the offices takes on the look of an outcrop of layers of sedimentary rock on the green hillside. The two stair towers push through the strata like volcanic cores and, to continue the geological analogy, the council chamber seems to have been plucked from the heart of the plan by seismic force, leaving behind the double height cubic void which makes up the entrance and exhibition space. This space, despite the play of levels and variety of vistas offered, is strangely reserved in mood with the major drama being reserved for the exterior. The entrance is flanked by the raised brick mass of the council chamber

References

Dungannon District Council offices. *RIBA Journal*, 87(8), 1980. 75.

Evans, D. Dungannon District Council Offices, Co Tyrone, Northern Ireland. *Architects' Journal*, 173(16), 1981. 743-754.

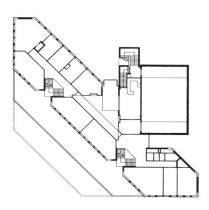

0 _____ 10

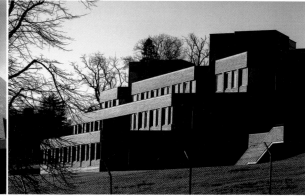

and by the approach stairs (propped on a cruciform column) and the massing of the broad interlocking volumes achieves a kind of lazy grandeur.

Appropriately, in the home of Tyrone Brick, this building is a masterclass in the crafting and detailing of brickwork. The stratified layers of offices are separated by glazing and each level oversails the lower by the width of half a brick. This sophisticated handling allows the layers to interlock, and the window mullions engage at differing levels like a giant brick zip-fastener. The stratification is again emphasised with bands of soldier courses which lace through the brickwork, internally and

externally, like hem-stitching. This interplay between inside and outside marks this building as an expression of brick sculpture in much the same way as the major buildings of Denys Lasdun can be read as sculptures in concrete. There is, too, a hint of Lasdun's work in the massing of the Council Offices which tumble out into the landscape in the manner of the University of East Anglia where the buildings themselves form the landscape. This building reinforces its topography and is built from the clay that belongs here.

Council offices are beacons of local democracy in the sea of direct rule that is Northern Ireland today; they are symbols

of local pride and also expressions of municipal rivalry between districts. There is nothing new in this, it was ever thus, but recent years appear to have lent a special edge to this rivalry and new council buildings are increasingly ambitious, even grandiose, in their design and lavish in their choice and range of materials. In this present climate Dungannon Council Offices appear reserved and somewhat understated but, over the years, the building's distinguished design has set the standard that other districts, and other architects, have tried to emulate. It received an RIBA Commendation in 1980.

Tollymore Tea House

NEWCASTLE   CO DOWN
IAN CAMPBELL & PARTNERS   1978

Tollymore Park had a considerable legacy of architectural interest before the arrival of this gem by Ian Campbell and Partners in 1979. The estate was described by the Gazetteer in 1787 as 'one of the most magnificently picturesque within the British dominions' and the sublime setting in the foothills of the Mournes featured an arboretum and generous planting of larches and oaks. Although the grand house has been demolished, the surviving buildings belong to 'the good no-nonsense robust Northern Irish vernacular tradition' according to the UAHS Mourne's listing. The entrances and Barbican gate are the more sophisticated early Gothick of the 18th century. The attenuated gate pillars

around the estate are known locally as Lord Limerick's follies.

The Teahouse is modestly scaled; a four square pavilion set in the landscape in the manner of those judiciously placed 'eye catchers' of the English landscape style of the 18th century. The 'Teahouse' title is a direct reference to the historical Japanese model which has been likened to 'a kind of inside-out sculpture of planes lines and textures'. These were constructed in timber with pitched roofs, elaborate eaves and exposed beam interiors. They were cool and astringent in character. The description could apply equally to Campbell's work. The setting, too, invokes the Japanese

connection; in Shinto mythology, the 'Kami' or gods are particularly associated with mountainous landscapes with forests, stones and waterfalls – the description again is apposite. There are other references at work here: at first sight the building suggests the work of some very advanced troupe of boy scouts who had raised their woodcraft to a highly sophisticated level and built a look-out post in the forest by lashing together a triangulated structure of timber poles. There is perhaps an echo, too, of the farm buildings of the northern European tradition in the Indian red timber sheeting, the piers of local granite and the dominant roof. These various threads and associations, however, come

together to establish a unique and very individual identity.

The building was commissioned by the Department of Commerce and the Department of Agriculture as a teahouse – an amenity for visitors in which afternoon teas were served during the summer months. The later arrival of campers and caravan owners on a nearby site required the redesign of the kitchen facilities to meet the greatly increased demands. The site was chosen by the client and is situated between the upper level car park, the site of the former grand house, and the lower park. The ground floor includes an ice cream shop, storage and toilets.

The first floor tearoom, a single volume, is approached by a bridge, which spans from the massive retaining wall of the upper car park, and by a staircase from below. The first floor slab is carried by an in situ concrete ring beam, supported at each corner by battered granite piers in squared random rubble, y-shaped in plan. Further support is provided by concrete columns midway between the piers and by weight bearing walls. The exterior walls are rendered in pebble dash.

The building, some 15 metres square, is canted in plan at a 45° angle to the line of the retaining wall so that none of the four glazed façades of the tearoom faces the

car-parking directly. This alignment sets up the kind of geometrical play of diagonals that Ian Campbell delights in. The roof form is a truncated pyramid with grey asbestos cement slating on 70mm timber sheeting which is carried on four pyramidal timber frames supported by a single central column and by eight free standing circular timber posts along the perimeter, which rise from ground level. At the heart of the plan an inverted pyramid forms the central flat roof and the enclosed space beneath houses the tank room and ventilation equipment. The interior woodwork, sheeting and beams, is stained red. Outside the primary structural zone a secondary system of triangulated

circular poles, bolted together, leans outward to carry the projecting roof and also to provide bracing to the primary structure. The secondary system also adds a 'layering' element to the façade – an intervening zone between inside and outside and it wittily transforms itself into the entrance bridge which originally spanned a small ornamental pool and reached down to a support at water level in mid-span. The pool has gone and with it something of the drama of entering the building.

At each corner, the overhanging roof is chamfered back to the column line which re-states the diagonal theme of the design and establishes an entrance motif at the entry point to the building by the raised, gable-like roof line that is formed. The roof also cuts back at the mid point of each façade, and here the rainwater chains hang from the guttering which run across the sections of cut out roof. (These chains have since proved ineffective in high wind and full height rainwater pipes have been inserted inside the chains.) The bridge breaks through an opening in the wall at the perimeter of the car park where two short ramps converge on the diagonal axis of the bridge which bisects the plan and sets up the symmetries within. The kitchen area – cooking, preparation and wash-up – is centrally placed and is flanked by serveries on each side. Two faceted 'cores' identical in form define each end of the kitchen area, these rise up in chunky red stained timber boarding with 'crenellated' profiles. One houses the cloakroom, toilets and lift and the other, the staircase to the ground floor level. The interior space of timber boarding stained red is artificially lit by clusters of globe lighting mounted on circular steel columns and the seating and tables are arranged about the perimeter space. The design shows the scrupulous regard for detail and the peculiar alchemy of geometry and structure that characterises Campbell's work – there is the suspicion that this can become a love of form for form's sake but here function and formalism combine to perfection.

References

Rankin, P. *The Mourne area of south Down.* Belfast: UAHS, 1975. 12-13.

Tea Tops. *Building Design,* (508), 1980. 8.

Tollymore Teahouse. *RIBA Journal,* 87(8), 1980. 45.

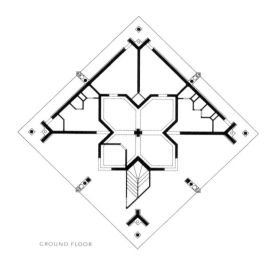

GROUND FLOOR

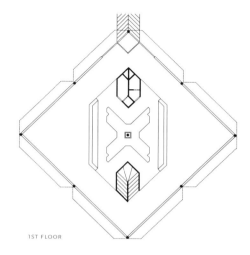

1ST FLOOR

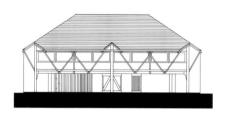

SOUTH EAST ELEVATION

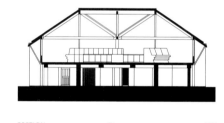

SECTION   0 ⌐_____⌐ 10

Tollymore Forest Park. *Plan*, 12(2), 1981. 30.

Tollymore Teahouse. *Architects' Journal*, 174(27), 1981. 65-74.

Tollymore Forest Park Teahouse. *AC Fibrecement Review*, 28(2), 1983. 46-48.

Jocelyn, Robert, Earl of Roden. *Tollymore: the story of an Irish demesne*. Belfast: UAHS, 2005.

Over the years the building has worn well and the exterior, despite limited maintenance, is virtually unchanged. It was particularly disappointing, therefore, to find it locked up and out of use on a visit in the summer of 2004. Changes in the building regulations have meant that certain aspects of its design no longer meet current legislation for public buildings. Access for the disabled presented considerable difficulties and the relationship of the kitchen area and the toilet was unsatisfactory. There is, it seems, no easy solution to these and other problems and the Forestry Service, which is now responsible for the building, has been forced to close it. It would be a sad day, indeed, if a building of such distinction were to be lost to Ulster architecture. The playfulness and human scale brought a new expression of Modernism to public awareness. The Teahouse received an RIBA Award in 1980; this was a national award and the Teahouse was one of only seven buildings in the United Kingdom which were honoured in that year. (The present system of national and regional awards was introduced by the RIBA in 1988). In the same year the Teahouse received a Civic Trust Commendation to be followed by an An Taisce Award in 1984.

It has been proposed that an architectural competition should be held to look into how the building could be brought into line with the legislation and also to examine the feasibility, if necessary, of adapting it for a new use, such as an educational resource or as a corporate venue for seminars, meetings and social purposes.

Architect's Own House

LISBELLAW   CO FERMANAGH
RICHARD PIERCE   1984

The house that Richard Pierce designed for himself reads like the return of the native, the affirmation of local tradition and the vernacular in a countryside under threat from the anonymity of 'bungalow bliss'. It also marks the architect's homecoming after years of study and practice abroad. Pierce is very much a son of Fermanagh where he grew up and went to school. He studied architecture in Edinburgh at the College of Art where the works of Louis Kahn and Robert Venturi were an inspiration. His interest in these architects, that he calls the Philadelphia School, drew him to America where he worked during his student vacations and for some years after graduating. He returned to Ulster in 1974 and from the outset he was actively engaged in building conservation, as a committee member of the UAHS, lecturing on local architecture and arguing the case for a better appreciation of our built heritage.

His own house is firmly rooted in tradition and if at first sight it seems like a riposte to Modernism, it embraces the Modernism of Robert Venturi.

Sometime before building this house Pierce had considered converting a Victorian schoolhouse as his home. It consisted of a single classroom with entrances at each end. Nothing came of the venture but the seed was sown and the idea of a multi-use space took hold and led to this building. The organisation of the plan follows Louis Kahn's separation of spaces into 'served' and 'servant'; here the large central 'served' space, the living/dining room, is flanked by the kitchen with store above on one side and, on the other, by the bedrooms and bathrooms – the 'servant' spaces. It is a rectangular block with rendered walls and slated roof; the clean cut gable and eaves treatment has the simplicity and economy that belongs to

traditional farm buildings. The bay window distinguishes this building as a dwelling and also the coloured 'strapwork' surrounds to the windows which are usually associated with the Scots tradition or that of north east Ulster. However Pierce, like a chef, has mixed together many ingredients in this design; in conversation he cited the influence of Alan Gailey's seminal work *Rural houses of the north of Ireland* which is especially evident in the design of the interior.

The full height dining/living room with its white walls, open hearth and boarded ceiling recalls the traditional farmhouse kitchen (although in this instance the kitchen is detached). The dining area can be seen as a re-working of the 'outshot bed' feature of the farmhouses of the west of Ireland where the thatched roof is carried out over a projection of the outside wall, beside the hearth, to form a sleeping recess.

References

Gailey, A. *Rural houses of the north of Ireland*. Edinburgh: John Donald Publishers Ltd, 1984.

McKinstry, L. Architecture alive and well and living in Lakeland. *Ulster Architect*, October 1985. 11-13.

McKinstry, R. Country style; mix of foreign and local influences in a recently completed house in Northern Ireland. *Architects' Journal*, 181(1/2), 1985. 40-43.

Truesdale, D. *The life and works of Richard H. Pierce*. Dissertation for B.Arch., Department of Architecture, QUB, 2002.

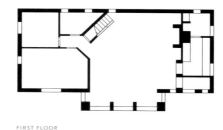

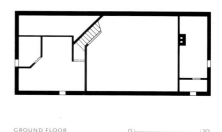

SECTION

FIRST FLOOR

GROUND FLOOR

0 _____ 10

The handling of the entrance porch echoes the 'hearth lobby' treatment of the vernacular house in which a visitor turns at right angles before entering the room, beside the fireplace. These two elements, the 'outshot' and the 'hearth lobby' are slight distortions of the traditional pattern but their ancestry seems apparent. Another influence cited by Pierce is Robert Venturi and the house for his mother at Chestnut Hill, Pennsylvania of 1962. Here the staircase does not take up a central position but it is nevertheless a major player in the principal space, slung across the corner of the room and establishing a diagonal axis towards the entrance. It is quirky and complex, rising behind a stepped wall upon which the steel purlin to the roof perches precariously. The signature flat segmental arches of Venturi's work are employed here: one spans the bay window opening and the other forms the arched recess to the fireplace.

To Robert McKinstry the room 'could well be some stylish art gallery or music room from almost any part of the world – despite the references to those old farm kitchen/living rooms – and a place of considerable tranquillity'. He noted the 'long generous bay window with its timber shutters and no curtains reminiscent of the simplest East Coast beach house' – another American reference. The design for the fireplace is based upon the fireplace for the boardroom of the Glasgow School of Art by Charles Rennie Mackintosh – the third major influence acknowledged by Pierce.

That influence is evident, too, in the elongated semi-circular garden wall which encloses the space in front of the living room, anchors the building to its setting and partially screens it from the road. This rough-cast wall recalls the walling at Windy Hill and the Hill House outside Glasgow; in this instance it is an echo of

those Iron Age and Early Christian hill forts which are a feature of the landscape – there is an example nearby. A pergola links the garden wall to the free-standing garage block at the approach to the house. This is constructed of creosoted telegraph poles supported by rough cast piers and it adds yet another 'imported' element to the design. Although the house was sold in 1995 and the kitchen extended to Pierce's designs, it remains the vision of one man; a kind of architectural testament or self portrait and, given the diversity of cultural references that are brought to bear, it is a very rich and multi-layered experience.

DE

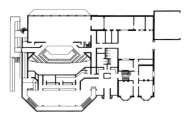

GROUND FLOOR

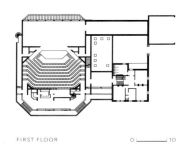

FIRST FLOOR   0 ⌊_____⌋ 10

Ardhowen Arts Centre

ENNISKILLEN   CO FERMANAGH
TOM MULLARKEY OF TRACEY & MULLARKEY   1987–8

The theatre, a low, glazed and faceted annexe to an existing country house, depends for its success and particular persona on a close relationship with the spectacular loughside setting. The choice of this site comes at a price, however, as the building is barely visible from the road and lacks 'civic' presence but the quality of the architectural experience it has to offer, more than compensates. The visitor comes across it as a delightful discovery.

Ardhowen House, an Edwardian villa, provides ancillary accommodation for the theatre, rehearsal rooms, office space and community facilities. The theatre is sited on the south side of the existing building and some excavation and re-grading of the adjacent drumlin was needed; seen from the lough the new theatre seems cradled in its gentle contours. The splayed profile

of the façade softens the impact of the new structure on the landscape and it also echoes the form of the traditional hipped roof of Ardhowen, its dormers too are echoed by the projecting ventilators to the theatre's roof. The slating on the new building matches exactly the Welsh slates of the old house. A strong horizontal binds old and new together, it runs at the level that glass meets slate on the theatre to join Ardhowen at eaves level. The massive portico which thrusts through the glass wall to the reception area is a transitional element between old and new and a reworking of the entrance porch to the house. Interplay is the essence of the design; the counterpoint of tradition and modernity, of mass and transparency and of natural landscape and high tech urbanity. The major player is the high glass wall to the public spaces. The green-tinted

glazing conveys an aqueous lakeland aura and the tall narrow panes recall something of the Victorian conservatory but the technology is cutting edge. It was designed by Billings Design Associates of Dublin, experts in curtain walling and consultants to leading Irish, and English, architects including Richard Rogers.

The entrance is marked by a sculpture, the work of a local artist, a flashback to the Viking long boats that marauded Lough Erne in the Dark Ages. Inside, the meticulously detailed front of house spaces are cool aquamarine experiences in soft blues and greens. The concrete-framed structure allows the low first floor slab to float free of the glass wall and two peripheral staircases rise through the interval between to meet at a central landing. The gradual ascent, along the glass wall, reveals

References

Ardhowen Arts Centre. *Ulster Architect*, January 1986. 5-6.

Orr, A.D. Building of the Year. *Ulster Architect*, November 1987. 4-6.

Triennial Gold Medal 1986-1988. *Irish Architect*, (98/99), 1993. 15.

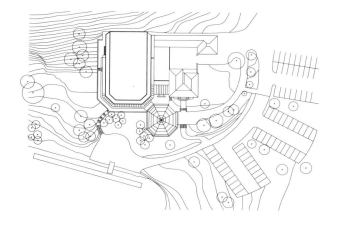

SIDE ELEVATION

FRONT ELEVATION

SECTION

a tableau of reed beds and lake water that suggests a painting by Terry Flanagan, the master of Fermanagh's landscapes.

The same peripheral circulation pattern applies inside the three hundred seater auditorium; the raked seating runs in an unbroken crescent from side to side and the aisles at each end connect directly with the stage at its own level. The interior achieves a lively consonance between audience and performers, and the same principle is at work in locating the actors' green room within vision of the foyer area.

The gestation period of this design was long and arduous; the theatre represents the culmination of a decade of effort by the Enniskillen Town Clerk, Gerry Burns, and the patience of Tom Mullarkey. The decision for the go ahead only came

through the injection of money from a European Community grant which required the drastic revision of the original scheme – it had included a five hundred seater auditorium. Such was the urgency that Mullarkey had to redesign the project in quick time. Looking back on those hectic days he concedes that the project may have benefited from the pruning and simplification required. It certainly possesses a lucid clarity. It has proved a commercial success as well; since its opening it has run at 70% capacity for the fifty weeks of the year it is open and there are current plans to upgrade the stage facilities through a mechanisation programme.

The building received an RIBA National Award in 1988 and was Ulster Architect's Building of the Year in 1987. The judge, Martin Pawley, architectural correspondent

of the Guardian, voted it as 'one of the best buildings' which he had seen in ten years. 'It rises to all the challenges', he continued, 'and by the brilliance of its own design conception adds others – it effortlessly matches modern and traditional materials and effortlessly marries itself to the existing building'.

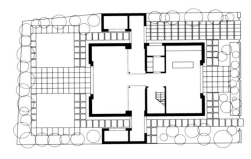

GROUND FLOOR

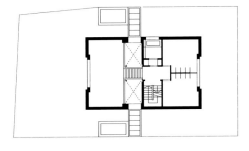

FIRST/SECOND FLOOR

Architects' Own House

BELFAST
W.A. AND J. HANNA   1988–96

The Malone area is perhaps the finest concentration of Victorian and Edwardian architecture in Ireland: recently it was declared a Conservation Area which should afford it some measure of protection from insensitive development. The pressures, however, are enormous and the last thirty years have seen the demolition of handsome Victorian villas and the erosion of its character by the appearance of developers Georgian, ill-judged Modernism and the building of four-storey apartment blocks.

This three-storey family house, designed for themselves by a husband and wife team, shows that Modernism at its best is perfectly compatible with the aims and objectives of Conservation Area legislation. At three storeys with rendered white walls and pitched roof, it conforms to its neighbours in scale, proportion and materials. These include some red brick inter-war houses and rough cast rendered buildings of the Arts and Crafts style. A crisply defined gable with window framed in steel sections and rising through three floors faces the road and establishes the building's Modernist pedigree. The eaves detailing, in which the rainwater guttering is carried on metal bracketing, again is sharp in definition and a nod perhaps to ornamental wrought-iron brackets which were a feature of the Arts and Crafts period.

The building evolved over a period of eight years being completed in 1996 and its design belongs to the high Modernism that conceived buildings as an assembly of volumes each serving a specific function. In this instance Louis Kahn's classification of spaces, as 'served and servant' controls the 'assembly of volumes'. To the east end of the building, facing the road, the bedrooms, bathrooms, kitchen and stairs are grouped as servant spaces to the living, dining and studio spaces to the west. These are approached at first and second floor levels by a bridge which spans the atrium which cuts across the plan at right angles and rises to the roof. It boldly demarcates the hierarchy of space and provides a lofty and striking entrance hall to the house, which can be approached from either side. The car parking is situated to the north and pedestrians approach from the south. The narrow atrium is fully glazed at each end and the interior is

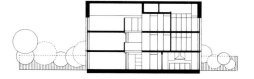

0 ⊢————————⊣ 10

flooded with natural daylight. The second floor studio space rises to the roof which is carried on white painted roof trusses in steelwork, and the end wall (a restatement of the gable which faces the roadway) with large areas of glazing surveys the Belfast hills to the west. The exterior wall finish is carried through into the white and luminous interior and the gable elevation reappears internally in outline as the wall that rises through the atrium and separates the two classifications of function.

Discipline and geometry pervade the design; it is as clean and ordered as a Bauhaus project but one has to look further afield than Modernism for other influences that shaped this project. The appeal of symmetry is eternal, it has informed architecture

throughout the ages as a means of establishing order and legibility. The Modern Movement may seem to have rejected the kind of certainties that symmetry has to offer but the works of Le Corbusier, for example, reveal a use of classical references and Renaissance ideals. In this house in south Belfast, Modernism engages with classical symmetry in a striking combination. The principal axis which runs longitudinally linking the gables with the central bedroom corridor and the bridge is marked externally by a vertical steel stanchion which interrupts the brickwork boundary wall to the roadway. A device that belongs to architects' architecture perhaps but a husband and wife team should be permitted some self-indulgence in designing their own house. The twin

approaches to the house, to left and right with storage spaces and glazed porches, maintain the sense of symmetry. These are aligned on the cross-axis defined by the atrium space and the two axes of the plan meet where the bridges span the void, bringing equilibrium and balance to the heart of the plan.

Glenveagh School

BELFAST
KENNEDY FITZGERALD & ASSOCIATES   1990–2

This special needs school, for 150 pupils both junior and senior, came into being with the merger of two schools in west Belfast, Glenravel and Iveagh, and relocation in the 'leafy suburbs' of south Belfast. The single-storey structure is very much at home in its suburban setting where it forms part of a campus with Fleming Fulton School with which it shares playing fields. Glenveagh School was designed by the same firm of architects and won an RIBA Commendation in 1986. In his account of the design, project architect Paddy Acheson referred to the 'airiness and negotiability' of the building, achieved by 'the use of courtyards and extensive roof glazing' in a deep plan, which was a marked departure from the earlier school designs of this practice, such as Victoria College Belfast, recipient of an RIBA Commendation 1973, and the

Collegiate School Enniskillen, an RIBA Award winner in 1969. In these projects classroom wings, dining areas and assembly halls were detached from one another to frame exterior spaces and define routes as small scale exercises in urban design.

At Glenveagh the deep plan is again adopted and the large single-storey school can be seen as a kind of mother ship moored on Harberton Park. Although the footprint of the building is roughly rectangular the underlying geometry of the plan is more complex – each structural bay of 10 metres recedes by 3 metres from the next to produce staggered façades in which each classroom is given individual expression. There are some striking benefits from this design strategy which creates incident and intimacy of scale. The façade to Harberton

Park ripples along in a busy sequence of covered play areas, each set back from the next. The projecting roof is carried by free-standing umbrella forms in tubular steel which also support the projecting valley gutters and 'Toblerone' roof lights. The masonry blockwork classroom walls rise and fall in raking and stepped profile, punctuated by full height glazing and large porthole windows. The stepped grid also brings diversity and drama to the internal spaces of the school.

The 10 metre structural grid derives from the classrooms which are spanned on the long axis by trussed portal frames, elegant and spare in tubular steel and the entire structure is detailed with great finesse. The roof form, an undulating progression of valleys and ridges with roof lights, runs transversely across the plan from side to

References

Designing a special needs school. *Architects' Journal*, 197 (13), 1993. 45-54.

Glenveagh School, Harberton Park, Belfast. *Ulster Architect*, 10 (4), 1993. 5-6, 56.

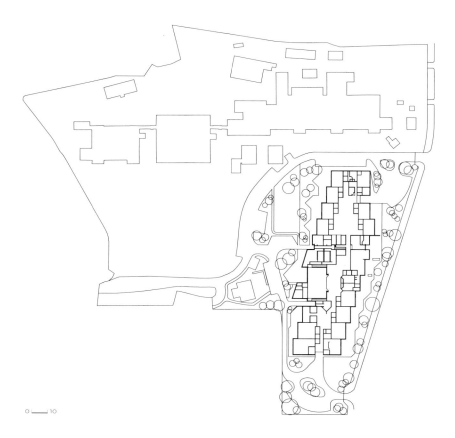

side and the interior seems to assume the persona of a single spatial entity within which the varying functions are lightly etched and defined by screen walls and glazing.

The school is approached from both ends, by juniors from the west and by seniors from the east. From each entrance hall the internal central space, or social concourse area, widens as it extends like a river delta; the two convergent spaces meet at a central transverse mall which divides the school into two halves. This space, with arched roof members and a fully glazed roof, gives access to medical and therapy rooms and a large special unit which are common to both sides of the school. The central circulation areas allow social interaction and group activities to take place in the vicinity of the classrooms. A longitudinal roof light slaloms its way above

these spaces, rising and falling and meeting the transverse roof lights at right angles. Ancillary accommodation, toilets, stores and utility rooms flank the concourse to provide sound insulation between teaching and circulation areas. The sound insulation in the ceilings is protected by perforated steel sheeting.

In the junior school the social concourse area is multi-functional, the widest expanse beside the gymnasium combines the varied functions of concourse, dining area and also, on occasions, a stage when the gymnasium takes on the function of an auditorium. The gym is sited at a lower level than the dining/concourse area and a large opening in the long wall provides a proscenium arch to the slightly raised 'stage' area. The specific spatial requirements of the gym mean that it does not conform

with the structural programme of the remainder of the building. However, it establishes an attractive cross-rhythm and point of emphasis at the heart of the plan.

This colourful, lively and animated building received an RIBA Commendation in 1993; at its opening the principal, Kay Murphy, reported that the children 'greeted the new school with delight' and she commented, at a visit by members of the UAHS, that parents had told her that it made their children feel valued.

DE

Ormeau Baths

BELFAST
TWENTY TWO OVER SEVEN   1990–6

This heart-warming project saved a much loved and fondly remembered Victorian building and brought it back into the public domain at a time when there was little optimism for such projects and economic depression was in the air. Its successful completion in 1996 provided, in Linda Brooks' words 'an invaluable inherited resource, offering strands of both physical and emotional continuity for Belfast'. The project required the refurbishment of both the interior and exterior of the old building and the addition of new wings to east and west. The first phase now provides office accommodation for the Health Promotion Agency of the

DHSS and an attic studio for twenty two over seven; these are situated in the west wing. The second phase, to the east, houses the galleries and offices of the Ormeau Baths Gallery – a contemporary arts space.

Opinions have varied as to the best approach to adding new work to an old building; to some the seamless extension of the old fabric is the best way forward while to others, including William Morris founder of the Society for the Protection of Ancient Buildings in 1895, new work should be of its time and should be clearly identified as such. The best architects, from Michelangelo to Michael Hopkins,

have always shown a spirit of respect for buildings of the past (Michelangelo's scheme for the Capitol in Rome is one instance and the extension of the Mound Stand at Lord's Cricket Ground, London, by Michael Hopkins, is another). Both retained elements of the historic structures and both extended the projects in their own style to form an integrated whole.

The two wings that twenty two over seven have added are in a modern idiom but are tempered by a sense of heritage and history. Both wings, which were built at different times, share the low barrel-roof form. This was a much favoured feature

References

Ormeau Baths.
Ulster Architect, 8(7), April/
May 1992. 15-16.

Brooks, L. Water wings.
Perspective, 4(1), 1995. 18-25.

Latimer, K. A choice building:
Ormeau Baths. *RSUA Yearbook*,
1996. 65-66.

Tipton, G. (ed). Space:
architecture for art. Dublin:
Circa, 2005. 168.

GROUND FLOOR

SECTION

0 ——— 10

of the architecture of the time but there are, too, echoes of the Belfast truss profile – curved lattices which were pioneered in this city. In both instances the gable profiles are edged by corbel courses of brickwork to form cornices and both tympanums feature circular windows.

In the west wing this feature makes 'eye-contact' with the ox-eye window, an oeil-de-boeuf, which decorates the pediment of Belfast's City Hall at the other end of Linenhall Street. Using red-clay brick, with raked joints to differentiate old from new, the vocabulary derives from the industrial and architectural heritage of the

area. The west elevation is arcaded with brick piers alternating with louvered panels set flush with the brickwork; these break through the plinth to reveal a cross-section of the massive bull nosed string-course which caps it. This massive profile reappears at cornice level above the giant concrete lintels which span between the piers. The weight and gravitas of these elements anchor the building firmly in the grain and texture of the buildings of this, the Linen Quarter of Belfast. They contrast with the festive spirit and jaunty air of the Queen Anne Revival Ormeau Baths. Extensive work was carried out on both the exterior brickwork and interior finishes in

the refurbishment programme, executed with loving care and diligence. The new east wing, home of the gallery, combines with the existing pool hall to form a sequence of luminous spaces which are ideal for the display of contemporary art. The building received an RIBA Award in 1998 and won the inaugural Royal Society of Ulster Architects Award in the same year.

DE

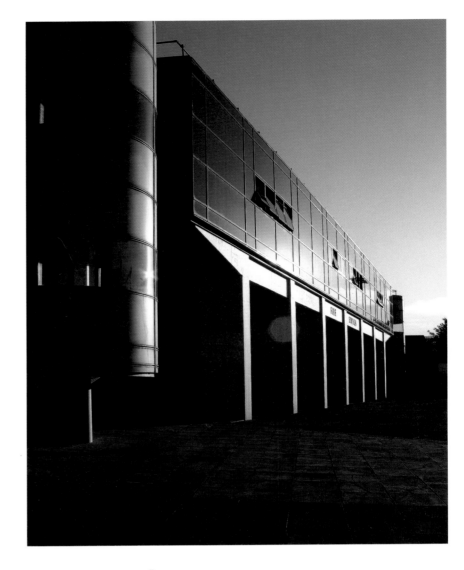

Eastern Area Command HQ
& Central Fire Station

BELFAST
KENNEDY FITZGERALD & ASSOCIATES   1991–5

The building takes the form of an open-sided courtyard which is framed on one side by a service wing and on the other two by the main elements of the programme which look out towards Ormeau Avenue in one instance and towards Ormeau Road in the other. The enclosed space is used for the cleaning, maintenance and servicing of the fire engines and it provides a training area with a drill tower as well as staff car parking. The Ormeau Avenue wing provides garaging for up to six firefighting appliances and, above the firemen's dormitory, presents a sleek façade in black glass. The significance of circulation is articulated by the towers

which rise at each end of the block, their silver and glass semi-cylinders contain the staircases and the firemen's poles.

A Divisional Headquarters such as this has a public role in consultation and education as well as its normal firefighting duties. A lofty entrance foyer to Ormeau Avenue leads to a first floor suite of interview and consultation rooms, the Fire Prevention Unit and offices for the Divisional Commander and his staff. These overlook the former Gas Offices on one side and, on the other, a balcony to the courtyard provides a vantage point for supervision of training and maintenance. At ground

floor in this administration wing, a central corridor leads to the kitchen and canteens on one side and to the kit rooms on the other which face the yard.

Siting played a major part in determining the character of this important building: the nearby Ormeau Baths and Gasworks Offices indicate the civic ambitions of this area of central Belfast in Victorian times. They are the work of Robert Watt and were built between 1887 and 1889 in red brick with carved ornamentation. The Fire Station, built a century later, shares these ambitions and revels in the same sharp detailing and modelling of its red clay

References

On fire. *Ulster Architect*, 10(2), 1992. 36-38.

Fired with enthusiasm. *Perspective*, 1(3), 1993. 28-30.

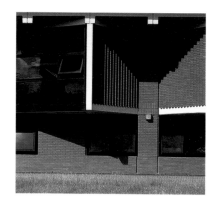

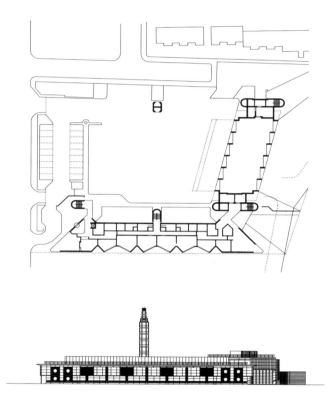

brickwork. The campanile-like drill tower with its metal crown is an attractive modern counterpoint to the gasworks' clock tower nearby. The other determining factor in the design was the configuration of the site itself. It is trapezoidal in shape which generated the lively geometry and play of angles which animate the building. The garaging block for example is a parallelogram in plan as it aligns with Ormeau Avenue. (The tapering forms used are also a reference to the pointed and rounded form of the Gas Offices at the point where the course of the Blackstaff once sliced across that site.) The administration wing presents a long façade to Ormeau Road. It 'concertinas' along in alternating planes of darkened glass and glowing red brickwork, rippled with chevron detailing. The roof slab, carried on paired cantilevered beams, tapers to a slim edge and at each end of the block it sweeps round the glazed corner in a pirouette that recalls the Expressionism of Erich Mendelsohn's architecture of the 1920s and 30s in Germany.

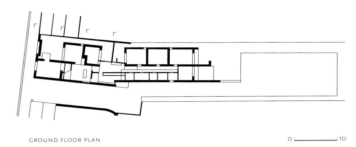

GROUND FLOOR PLAN

0 ⌞_____⌟ 10

Glenavy Surgery

GLENAVY   CO ANTRIM
TIM RONALDS & (POST-CONTRACT) MCCREANOR & LAVINGTON   1992

Sited in a rural village, this local surgery exhibits an unpretentiousness that teaches much about the modesty, scale and practicalities of our rural building culture. Despite its discreet presence, this building makes an important contribution to Ulster's recent architectural landscape since it makes reference to the vernacular whilst avoiding a sentimental approach. It demonstrates a considered Modernism engaging successfully with its established surroundings without any sense of inappropriateness or awkward juxtaposition. Through the understated qualities of its single-storey whitewashed forms, it attains an almost invisible quality fitting naturally into the street without over-emphasising its newness.

The building presents itself to the street as a plain rendered wall and is entered through a simple portal, set asymmetrically to one side of the narrow frontage. This portal gives access to a tiny forecourt that provides a significant sense of detachment from the street as one passes into the building. This sequence, minor as it is, distinguishes the building's semi-public nature from nearby houses and shops that are accessed directly from the pavement.

The plan is organised in a linear form stretching into the deep plot that runs perpendicular to the street. The scale of the forecourt establishes the pattern of organisation for the whole project where the interrelation of small 'room-like'

external courts interact with the internal spaces creating a relaxed and friendly environment that seems so suited to the idea of well-being. The inclusion of a fireplace in the reception/waiting area gives a homely feel to a routine visit to the doctor in a simple way. Similarly, a low-level window beside the nurses' room is designed for children to look through into one of the little gardens. These courtyard gardens are enclosed by manipulating the boundary timber fencing (detailed to appear more wall-like in character) so that it extends to, and provides cladding for, the adjacent surfaces of the surgery walls and combines with the main plan to create a series of intimate indoor-outdoor relationships.

References

Jenkins, D. Surgical precision. *Architects' Journal*, 195 (20), 1992. 24-27.

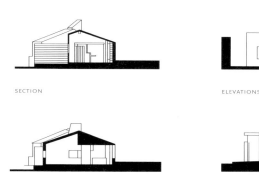

SECTION

ELEVATIONS

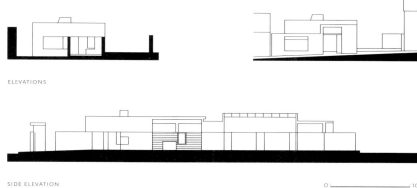

SECTION

SIDE ELEVATION

0 _____ 10

A kink on plan allows the building to follow the line of the boundary in a straight-forward way and signals a point beyond which the treatment rooms and ancillary accommodation are organised around a top-lit corridor; the mass of the building is broken at this junction with the roof level dropping to maintain an appropriately modest scale. At the tail end of this arrangement, the last consulting room and the staff room overlook a garden with the car park beyond. The route from the car park back past the length of the building allows the visitor to experience it as a collection of spaces, deftly articulated to respect the suitably low-key scale of development and thereby ensuring an institutionalised environment is avoided.

Local surgeries such as this one have been encouraged over recent years through the incentive of loans structured specifically for general practitioners. While many surgeries were built under the loans scheme, this one stands out for its sensitivity and appositeness to mid-Ulster's building tradition. Apparently simple yet with a delicacy in the planning and detail, this building demonstrates, through its design, a tender and very human quality at work. Whilst its Modernist credentials are easily traced, it never feels far removed from the traditional home and hearth.

AH

Blackwood Golf Centre

BANGOR   CO DOWN
O'DONNELL & TUOMEY   1992–4

The Blackwood Golf Centre echoes the traditional clustered patterns of Irish agrarian building. It can be read as a collection of discrete forms collected together and built onto what the architects have described as a 'constructed landscape'.

The degree of cultivation of the landscape intensifies from the surrounding wooded hills through farmland on to the golf course itself before culminating in the construction of terraces, cuttings and embankments around the building. Most prominent of these features is the car park which is laid out over a series of terraces that work across the natural contours and gently drop down towards the main entrance portico (a roofed space between the restaurant/bar block and the main reception area) which, in turn, gives onto an elevated courtyard. The generous arc of the driving range canopy defines the edge of this space whilst visual connections with both the 1st tee and the 18th green reassert the notion of a complete circle around the course and landscape.

The complex appears at first to be a modest cluster of rural buildings taking their inspiration from agricultural sheds but on closer inspection can be seen to have the qualities of a small urban composition with the conscious structuring of landscape having formal undertones. This latent sense of formality pervades the project, elevating its status above its agricultural point of reference and bringing a sense of social purpose to its spaces. The large open veranda to the bar responds to the scale of the distant view and lends an Arcadian dignity to the golf course.

The complex is split into a number of component parts, each identified and resolved through a distinct building

References

O'Toole, S. Blackwood Golf Club. In Becker, A. Olley, J. and Wang, W. (eds). *20th century architecture: Ireland.* Munich & New York: Prestel Verlag, 1997. 186-187.

O'Donnell and Tuomey Architects. *Scroope VI (Journal of the Cambridge University School of Architecture),* 1993-94. 58-59.

Blackwood Golf Centre. *Irish Architect*, 107, 1995. 30-32.

Ryan, R. Arcadian greens. *Architectural Review*, 198 (1186), 1995. 75-77.

O'Regan, J. (ed). *O'Donnell + Tuomey. (Architecture profile, 1)*. Kinsale, Gandon Editions, 1997.

element. Whilst not especially peculiar to Ulster, these 'sheds' integrate easily into the landscape with a reassuring familiarity but now set to new purpose. The largest of these, facing west over the 18th green, houses the restaurant and bar and presents the most formal elevation to the landscape. To the east lie the reception area, changing facilities and shop in front of a bridge giving access to the 1st tee through the woods. Other facilities are handled through a basement that is cut in underneath the primary courtyard level. The building has undergone some modifications and the initial allocation

of functions mentioned above has not been maintained; nonetheless it remains largely unspoilt.

The poetic qualities of the project are developed further through its use of materials. A palette of predominantly natural materials (untreated cedar, terne-coated steel and red pigmented plaster) is explored through various combinations that allow each element of the building to express a distinct presence. The natural ageing of these materials has allowed the building to mellow and relax into the site with the distinction between the cultivated

landscape and the architecture becoming appropriately blurred.

The architects' efforts to achieve a certain 'civic informality' have succeeded with a rich interaction of space, landscape, building, materials and people characterising this project. Whilst having a very specific function, this building also has much to teach us about building in the countryside.

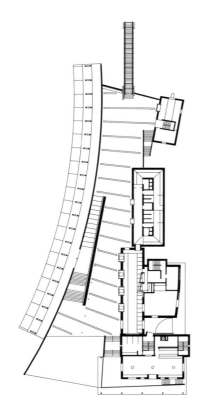

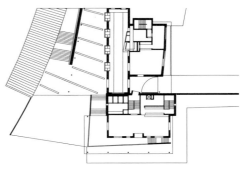

SECTION   GROUND FLOOR   FIRST FLOOR   0 ⎣_____⎦ 10

Rail & Road Transport Galleries

CULTRA CO DOWN
IAN CAMPBELL & PARTNERS   1992–5

These conjoined galleries, designed to house substantial parts of the Ulster Folk and Transport Museum's collection, were built in two phases, the Rail Transport Gallery in 1992-3, and the Road Transport Gallery in 1993-5. Built on a steeply sloping site in a pleasant parkland setting, the buildings comprise a very large vaulted hangar-like exhibition space of rectangular plan – the Rail Transport Gallery – linked by a narrow angled bridge to a reception block on a higher level, and by a broad lobby to another vaulted but T-shaped block – the Road Transport Gallery – downhill from it.

The first of the two, the Rail Transport Gallery, was designed to accommodate the museum's comprehensive Irish railway collection which covers the whole of Ireland. Its barrel-vaulted shape, with soaring gables

and radiating gable members, was consciously influenced by the great Victorian railway stations of the past, deliberately echoing the 'age of steam', while the building's particular siting was determined by a connection to the main Belfast to Bangor railway line. This spur line is actually incorporated into the gallery itself, terminating in a circular turntable which forms the centrepiece of the exhibition space. Train exhibits can thereby be transported into the building by rail, with the turntable being used to connect with the various display lines inside.

Construction of the gallery is of curved tubular space-frame trusses which spring from a base of blue engineering bricks – such brick being appropriate in the engineering context and visually suitable

to provide a heavy base for the off-white structural deck – to span thirty-five metres and support the roof of embossed aluminium panels which were profiled and curved on site and crimped into position.

The main entrance, in the form of a pair of identical doorways, is in the reception block, a small single-storey building of quirky form, set at an angle, which contains a small audio-visual theatre and ancillary rooms. Its aluminium roof follows the same radius curve as the gallery roof, set diagonally on the square plan, the exposed V-shaped space-frame truss in the foyer giving a foretaste of the structural forms that lie beyond the linking bridge. From the elevated glazed bridge is visible the spur line railway track which leads in through the side of the main gallery at ground level,

References

Transports of delight. *Perspective*, 1 (5), 1993. 32-40.

Building study: space to display rolling stock. *Architects' Journal*, 198 (2),1993. 35-45.

Project profile: Cultra shock. *Brick Bulletin*, Winter 1999. 12-14.

On the road again. *Perspective*, 4 (3), 1996. 16-25.

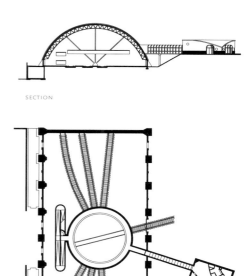

SECTION

GROUND FLOOR   0 ———— 10

the bridge itself entering the gallery at a much higher level, its height having been determined by the clearance required by the largest exhibit, all achieved by clever use of the natural slope of the land.

Inside the main museum shed, some of the grandeur of 19th century engineering achievements is recaptured in the large size and evocative form of the vaulted space, the crisp precision of details, and the impressive structural display. A series of V-shaped space-frame trusses are used to carry flexible air ducts across the roof and support the soaring hoops of gable glazing which provide not only a dramatic element but also a welcome relief in an otherwise artificially lit space. The connections between the gable trusses and the radial posts were made demountable

to allow for possible extensions in the future. The elevated link from the entrance building connects directly with a circular gallery which follows the curve of the turntable below and permits views down over the trains as if from a railway bridge; from that level a ramp descends to the main floor level. Bridge, viewing gallery and ramp were all constructed of cast in situ reinforced concrete with an exposed aggregate finish.

The Road Transport Gallery takes the form of a two- and three-storey extension to the rail gallery and continues the development on down the sloping site. It exhibits the collection of trams, cars, motorcycles, bicycles and public service vehicles. It is clearly related to the earlier gallery yet distinctly different. Whereas the rail gallery

flamboyantly demonstrates contemporary technology, the road gallery pays respect to Belfast's Victorian past. Brickwork is the main material both inside and outside, blue engineering bricks being used in the upper level to provide a visual link with the earlier building, whereas at lower level red brick is used, while the segmental forms of the roof and gable openings, as well as the steel 'pseudo Belfast trusses', are also reminiscent of the same great age of local industrial archaeology.

Amongst other awards the Rail Transport Gallery gained an RIBA Regional Award in 1993, while the Road Transport Gallery gained a commendation from the RIAI in 1997.

Waterfront Hall

BELFAST
ROBINSON & MCILWAINE   1992–6

The Waterfront Hall is the centrepiece of the redevelopment of Belfast's riverside intended to link the city centre with the long-neglected River Lagan, but the building has a wider significance. Conceived as far back as 1978 when Belfast was suffering badly from the effects of terrorism and civil strife, the idea behind it was not just to create a useful cultural complex but also to try to instil a spirit of confidence in the future of the city and improve its image abroad. Its success in achieving this has made it the symbol and icon of the 'new' Belfast.

Designed in 1992 by the firm of Robinson and McIlwaine and completed by 1996, this was not only the first major civic building

in Belfast since the 1930s, but the first in the 20th century to be designed by local architects. It takes the form outside of a large circular drum clad in Portland stone, red brick and granite, with a vast expanse of glazing, all crowned by a low copper-covered domical roof. Joined to one side is a minor hall of lower height and rectangular plan. Despite the suggestion of such classical elements as pilasters and entablature, and allusions to the past in its range of masonry and roofing materials, the overall expression is entirely modern, with an abstract feel, underlined by the Hi-Tech planar glazing canting out toward the river, and the angular porte-cochère at the entrance. The large areas of glazing impart a higher

degree of transparency to a civic building than usual, revealing much of the activity within and thus ensuring an inviting view from outside.

There was no one reason for the cylindrical form which arose from a combination of aesthetics, function and site, but it was a happy choice. Its formality expresses its civic nature and sets it apart from the commercial buildings of office blocks and hotel around it, while the circular shape makes for an economical way of wrapping foyers and ancillary rooms around the auditorium.

Inside, the circular form of the exterior has created interesting three-dimensional

References

Bravo: Belfast Waterfront Hall. *Perspective*, Special Edition, January 1997.

Building study: on the waterfront. *Architects' Journal*, 205(9), 6 March 1997. 35-41.

Belfast belle. *World Architecture*, (57),1997. 118-119.

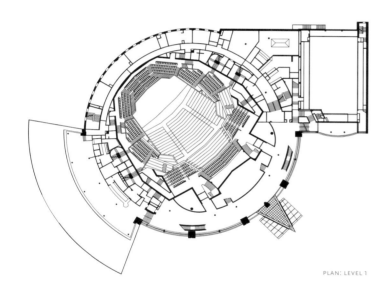

PLAN: LEVEL 1

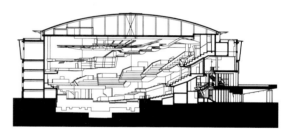

SIDE ELEVATION   0 ⌞_____⌟ 10

volumes and shapes in the front-of-house areas where the curved foyers are juxtaposed with the stairways, while the setting back of the upper foyers to produce a three-storey void has enhanced the sense of spaciousness and established an exciting visual relationship between floor levels. These public spaces include a restaurant, café and bars, as well as an exhibition gallery. Detailing is crisp and modern, with stainless steel fittings, Spanish marble surfaces to foyer floors and stairways, and laminated glass bridges on steel structural supports leading from an upper level to the main auditorium.

At the heart of the building, and totally enclosed, is the massive 2250-seat auditorium with floors that can be raised and lowered for a range of musical performances and other events with the added flexibility of moveable stall seating. The fixed seating layout follows the pioneering example established by Hans Scharoun at Berlin's Philharmonic Hall, with a 'terraced vineyard' arrangement comprising symmetrically disposed interlocking 'boxes' which each seat between 35 and 80 people, providing excellent acoustics and sight-lines throughout the hall. A noticeable absence of intervening columns adds to the grandeur and indeed the drama of this vast interior space. The domical form of roof outside is, however, not expressed inside the hall, the building's location below the flight path to the nearby City Airport necessitating a double-skin concrete roof for sound protection. From the flat auditorium ceiling hang concentric rings of acoustically reflecting and diffusing panels whose circular shapes recall the building's exterior drum-like form.

The Clachan

MAGHERAFELT CO LONDONDERRY
TWENTY TWO OVER SEVEN 1994

This small cluster of four houses in Magherafelt occupies 'the delicate margin where town meets farmland'. Its neighbours on the site are the usual suburban stylistic mix of North American-style bungalows and mock-Tudor and mock-Georgian villas but this speculative housing development by Gribbin Construction is both modern in spirit and also firmly rooted in the indigenous rural building tradition. The word 'clachan' is the Irish for the small hamlets of farm buildings that are associated with the ancient open-field system of land utilization. Such was the apparently random nature of their layout that in the words of one 19th-century writer, they appeared to have fallen 'in a shower from the sky'. Once the centres of communal life and tradition, they survived until the mid-19th century. The traditional isolated farmhouse is a relatively recent and post-famine arrival in Ulster's countryside. This housing development has something of both these antecedents. The differing alignments of the blocks and the convergent angles between their units suggest the layout of a clachan and the pitched slated roofs, white rendered walls and gate pillars belong to the traditional Ulster farmhouse and outbuildings.

From the top of the sloping site the visitor is presented with a descending sequence of roofs and gables at right angles to one another. Each house is made up of two nearly parallel blocks of the same size, living rooms in one and bedrooms in the other. They are single room in width and connected by a glazed entrance lobby – this central space is crucial as it allows the traditional forms, which the design employs, to be re-interpreted as modern interiors. Long corridors are unnecessary and the living area flows as one spatial experience from end to end. Two blocks run parallel to the contours of the site and bedrooms occupy the lower unit which is two storied; the other two houses cut across the slope and bedrooms are accommodated in the lower end of each unit which rise to two floors.

References

Otway, C. A tour in Connaught: comprising sketches of Clonmacnoise, Joyce country and Achill. Dublin: W.Curry & co,1839. 353.

Evans, E. Irish folkways. London: Routledge & Kegan Paul, 1957. 29.

McGrath, Aidan. Urban housing in a rural tradition. Architects' Journal, 199(23), 1994. 43-51.

Department of the Environment for Northern Ireland. A design guide for rural Northern Ireland. Belfast: DOENI, 1994.

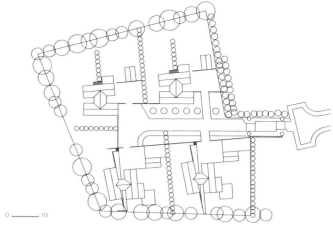

0 —— 10

TYPICAL SECTION

0 —— 10

TYPICAL ELEVATIONS

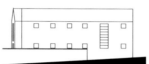
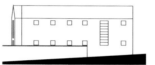

LOWER GROUND FLOOR

GROUND FLOOR & FIRST FLOOR PLAN

The exterior employs the vocabulary of the Ulster farmhouse; the elevations have the familiar balance of solid and void but the accent is modern. The solid chimney stack is here replaced by a stainless steel flue and the traditional sash window opening becomes a single sheet of glass. The detailing of the eaves follows the time-honoured rural pattern; it is direct and simple and it touches on the 'Functional Tradition' that Modernism has claimed as its own. Inside, the traditional hearth is re-cast as a free-standing monolith, occupying the heart of the plan and dividing the lounge from the dining area and partially screened kitchen. Timber king-post roof trusses are painted red and the roof

planes and walls white. Floor finishes are of high quality, in solid wood and polished porcelain.

The erosion of the quality of Ulster's countryside by insensitive housing development has been a growing cause for concern in recent years. The *Design guide for rural Northern Ireland* is just one of a series of publications to address the problem. It called for new buildings to be grouped about existing settlements, siting to respect existing landmarks and hedgerows and the design to reveal an informed use of traditional form and detail. The unique marriage of Modernism and the vernacular shown in this Magherafelt

housing scheme seems to have anticipated all these recommendations and shows that we can still build in harmony with the countryside. Rightly it has won many plaudits including an RIBA Housing Project Award in 1993 and a Royal Society of Ulster Architects Award in the same year.

DE

Irish Linen Centre

LISBURN   CO ANTRIM
CHAPLIN HALL BLACK DOUGLAS   1994

The early 1990s were witness to the continuing debate between modernity and tradition and the occasionally recurring struggle to reconcile the two, as context and location became ever more important aspects of design. The period also saw the rise of a new type of building, the interpretative centre, invented to serve the tourist industry. These two preoccupations came together at the Irish Linen Centre in Lisburn.

The Irish Linen Centre is an addition to an existing building – the old listed market house, largely of the 18th century but remodelled in the 19th – which had been adapted as the Lisburn Museum in the early 1980s. Rather than being treated as a subservient extension to this venerable old centrepiece of the Market Square, however, the new addition – required as a focus for the study and promotion of the linen industry in Ireland – was conceived as a new building in its own right.

The proportions of the old building were respected but no attempt was made to replicate its Italianate detailing, and although such recognisably historic features as arches, columns, parapets and pitched roof forms were adopted, they were treated in a contemporary way. This new three-storey block, comprising an in situ concrete frame, clad in smooth dressed sandstone, with small steelwork sections employed at high level, and featuring such Modernist elements as polished metal tubular railings and windows of both plate glass and glass blockwork, was linked to the old two-storey market house by means of a tall glazed atrium.

The atrium, which forms a common entrance for both the old market house museum and the new interpretative centre, is comprised of full-height planar glazing with heavy glass doors at either end, and contains an internal bridge at first floor

level linking the two buildings. The new and the old blocks were thus structurally connected but visually separated so that each could retain its individual identity.

In addition to the atrium entrances, the new building is also approached through the gable end which faces down the triangular Market Square. Originally recessed between two free-standing piers supporting an oversailing upper bay, but now enclosed in a porch, the front entrance leads into a high-ceilinged ground floor area housing a shop, originally intended to concentrate on high-quality linen goods, and a café, with a mezzanine platform originally intended for temporary exhibitions. Beyond toilets, kitchen accommodation, a public stairwell and a lift, lies the atrium.

The interior of the atrium is a creative mixture of past and present. Here the old and new meet. The plain smooth stone

References

The fabric of society. *Perspective*, 3(1),1994. 16-25.

MacNiece,D. The Irish Linen Centre Lisburn Museum. *Ulster Architect*, 11(10), 1994. 9-11.

Mairs, B. Modernism in an Irish town earns plaudits for sensitivity. *Architects' Journal*, 202(12), 1995. 34-35.

Graby, J. (ed). *Building on the edge of Europe*. Dublin: RIAI, 1996. 104-105.

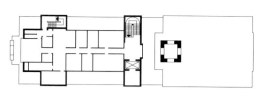

SECOND FLOOR

FIRST FLOOR

0 ———— 10

GROUND FLOOR

walling and modern lines of the new building along one side of the high lateral lobby faces the Italianate stuccoed end wall of the market house along the other side, the latter incorporating an extensive area of rubble stonework in the central tower now left exposed following the removal of adjoining buildings on the site, without any attempt to recreate an original classical façade. Recessed in the base of this exposed rubble wall is the new bow-fronted reception desk of beechwood, Baltic green granite, and stainless steel, the point from which a tour of both the museum and the interpretative centre begins.

The old building was retained almost unchanged, its ground floor containing the local museum, with its first floor – the former Assembly Rooms, restored by Robert McKinstry in 1980 – serving as a lecture room and space for temporary exhibitions. In the new building, the main interpretative display for the linen industry occupies the first floor, accessed by both a staircase of steel and polished wood from the ground floor, and the overhead bridge from the old building, while the basement contains stores and workshop facilities and an audio-visual display. The second floor is occupied by offices and archives.

Contemporary professional opinion judged the Irish Linen Centre 'an excellent example of the conjoining of an old and a new building to produce a coherent entity', adding that 'the challenge inherent in such a project has been successfully handled, each part contrasting with but not diminishing the other'. While some minor changes and unsympathetic later internal fittings and furnishings may detract from the original clarity of interior space, the overall achievement remains, and the value of contemporary architecture underlined. A modern building, handled with sensitivity, was inserted into an entirely traditional setting, at the epicentre of an historic town, and not only successfully transformed the image of its immediate locality but also helped raise the status of the town itself.

The Irish Linen Centre gained an RIBA Regional Award, an RIAI Regional Award, and a Civic Trust Award, all in 1995.

Architect's Own House

DERRYGONNELLY   CO FERMANAGH
RICHARD PIERCE   1995

Buildings such as this usually belong to the realms of fantasy like Yeats's 'small cabin' on the Lake Isle of Innisfree or to the architecture of the Earl Bishop of Derry, an aristocrat with a taste for the 'sublime'.

There are other instances of the pursuit of an idyll but this flight of fancy is a rare and delightful experience – timeless yet very much of its time. Architecture such as this requires the opportunity but it also calls for nerve on the part of the architect to go ahead and build it. Pierce held his nerve here but admits that his earlier project at Lisbellaw had also started life as a circle but at the time he 'did not have the courage to see it through'. The originality, audacity even, of this scheme which sets it apart, is to build an 'archaeological artefact', a ring fort in a ruinous condition, and then to inhabit it – a process that owes something to the behaviour of the hermit crab which inhabits the abandoned shells of gastropod molluscs.

The practice of building a ruin is nothing new. It was all the rage among wealthy landowners of the Age of Reason; their estates were dotted with sham Gothic ruins of abbeys, churches and hermitages as a way of improving the landscape quality by providing 'eye-catchers'. (Nothing built in Ireland can rival the 'Jealous Wall' a seventy foot high Gothic ruin built at Belvedere House, Mullingar, to blot out the view of a brother's house.) Pierce has based his sham ruin on the ring fort and in particular the circular stone walled enclosures known as cashels which represented a way of life that persisted from the late Bronze Age (circa 900 BC) until the Middle Ages. They were the houses of substantial farmers, or ranchers, and ranged in diameter from 20m to 70m with a dry stone wall from two to three metres in thickness. Small circular structures, houses or storage buildings, are found inside these enclosures; these were made of wickerwork or were stone built. The more sophisticated and grander

examples, such as Staigue Fort, Co Kerry or the Grianan of Aileach, Co Londonderry include an arrangement of stone stairways leading to walkways, and cells and galleries within the thickness of the battered walls. The finest of these stone forts are found on the Aran Islands where Dun Aengus is splendidly sited on a cliff top overlooking the Atlantic. At Derrygonnelly the rubble stone walls are girdled by carved string-courses which are a nod perhaps to the detailing of Plantation castles, an anachronistic touch that suggests we should not take things at face value.

The setting for Pierce's 'folly' is Arcadian and the views are sublime. The sloping site is generous and it overlooks Carrick Lake, complete with a crannog, a man-made island of the late Bronze Age; the backdrop is a wooded hillside. The ruined cashel, it must be said, is on the small side, at some 12m in diameter, but every effort has been taken to lend it verisimilitude, and when

References

Venturi, R. *Complexity and contradiction in architecture.* 2nd ed. London: Architectural Press, 1977.

Singmaster, D. Round house ancient model. *Architects' Journal,* 201(16),1995. 31.

Making history? *Perspectives on Architecture,* 6(1), 1997. 66-69.

Truesdale, D. *The life and works of Richard H. Pierce.* Dissertation for B.Arch., Department of Architecture, QUB, 2002.

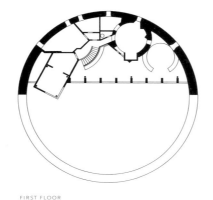

GROUND FLOOR   FIRST FLOOR   SECTION   0 ———— 10

time and weathering has softened its appearance it should look very much the part. The battered walls in Donegal sandstone, 1.3m in thickness, rise to 5m at their highest and reduce to waist height toward the south west to follow the descending lie of the land. The circle is bisected and the dwelling with mono-pitched roof and glazed wall running from side to side overlooks the courtyard at the lower level. Three open circles in whitewashed stone carve the interior into a sequence of varied and hierarchical spaces, in this instance 'master' and 'menial' – toilets and stores are squeezed into the interstitial spaces between the circles. The central space is multi-purpose, as at the earlier house at Lisbellaw, but here Pierce seems to have adopted the vision of William Morris (the self-styled inventor of the simple life, according to Osbert Lancaster); the ideal room, he declared, is one that includes working, sleeping, eating and cooking in one space.

The play of curved forms is indeed organic to the extent, as has been suggested, of recalling biological organs. The dominant element is the long promenade, which is the heart of the house; it presides over the courtyard and commands the prospect of lake and mountains in a 'seigneurial' manner like a lord of the manor. The long double glazed wall, with shutters, is interrupted by the two-storey study/ bedroom element which punches through it and rises above eaves level in a stark counterpoint to the curvilinear and Celtic flow of the interior. Pierce has used the phrase 'a latter-day British Army lookout post' in describing it. Its angularity skewers the plan to a fixed reference point and established a link between the internal and external space as it belongs to both. It also introduces a new world of reference, whereas the building could be seen as working within archaeological parameters, this canted geometry recalls the constructivist/ supremacist designs of Russia in the 1920s

and the work of Konstantin Malenkov and EL Lissitzky. The same diagonal astringency is evident in the reflecting pool in the paved and gravelled courtyard.

Architecture as idiosyncratic as this with its implied rejection of the orthodoxies and good manners of late Modernism can encounter a cool response from the architectural press. Pierce should take heart from Robert Venturi whose book, *Complexity and contradiction in architecture* is an attack on 'the limitations and orthodoxies of modern architecture (and city planning), in practice the platitudinous architects who invoke integrity, technology and electronic programming as ends in architecture'. Pierce is following Liam McCormick in striking a balance between Irishness and Modernity in this reworking of the Villa Rotunda idea.

Arttank Studio & Gallery

BELFAST
SIMON TEMPLETON 1998–2000

The gallery is located in a Victorian brick terrace on the Lisburn Road; to the rear and, separated from it by an access lane, is the studio. The hinterlands of these Victorian terraces in Belfast usually possess a distinctive character; litter-strewn and somewhat ominous, they hardly welcome the casual visitor and there is something of a clandestine air about the workshops and garages found there. The studio, a small brick tower, has a semi-industrial look. The building which formerly occupied the site when Bernard Jaffa, the gallery owner, bought it had been a motor-cycle factory, and was then in use as a coal-house. This structure was demolished. The architect's brief was very open-ended, in Jaffa's words it should be, 'a place for contemplation and an example of form without function and an essay in art for art's sake'.

The two-storey building in re-used brick with bull-nosed corners occupies a site where two lanes meet and presents a glazed entrance door to the outside world. Above, a full-height opening has the look of a loading bay which reinforces the industrial image of the small building. The interior belongs to that realm of high art where sophistication and the primitive meet head on. The ground floor is finished in concrete slabs, waxed and polished. The walls are finished in plastered bonding which, in normal practice, is a preparatory coat for the final smooth-skin finish. The plasterer was not told that this coat was to be the intended finish. The resulting finish is unstudied and casual and makes an excellent backdrop for the paintings – soft, grey and slightly porous-looking. The smooth plastered ceiling contains recessed fittings which bathe the walls in light. A

small recess facing the entrance rises as a double-height space, side-lit by glass blocks. The first floor is reached by a spectacular ribbon of plate steel which zigzags its way as it rises. This narrow staircase is supported minimally on steel cantilevers and touches neither the walls nor the ground floor. It is pared down minimalism. There are no balusters, simply a 25mm square handrail supported at top and bottom. The floor finish at first floor level is oak-boarding and the strips of hessian which act as balustrading are an art installation in themselves.

Since the building was completed, in 1998, a small toilet facility has been added. This, again, is slim-line minimalism and it is cantilevered from the side wall at first floor level. A new series of steps span the void and a sliding door (housed in the cavity of the

References

Hardcore. *Perspective*, 7(1), 1998. 37-41.

Weston, R. *Plans, sections and elevations : key buildings of the twentieth century.* London: Laurence King Publishing Ltd, 2004. 96.

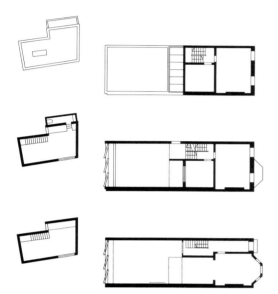

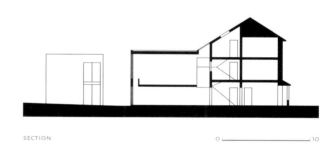

SECTION   0 ———————— 10

brick wall) gives access to the washroom. The raised, slatted floor in mahogany allows this tiny space to function as a shower. *Perspective* regarded this building as 'the kind of gallery prepared to show the work of artists at the cutting edge and to offer a match between the style and panache of its own construction'. The mood of rigorous severity may recall the domestic work of Tadao Ando, the Japanese architect, and there are also echoes of Luis Barragan's house and studio of 1947-8 in Mexico City which creates an 'abstract almost surreal world' and features a single minimal flight of stairs.The building received an RIAI Award in 1998 and, when visited, was let out as an office for an advertising agency.

The studio was phase I of the Arttank project; work started on phase II, the gallery which occupies the rear portion of the Victorian terrace, in 1999. The format of the traditional terrace features a return wing and yard to the rear. This wing was demolished and the new two-storey extension occupies the rear half of the site. Bernard Jaffa's dental practice is located in the first and second floors of the terrace house and the Arttank gallery takes up the entire ground floor space running from bay-windowed front to the glass brick rear wall which can be opened up as three centrally pivoted units. The gallery extension uses the same polished concrete floor finish and bonding plaster walls as the studio. Above, the reception area to the dental surgery is an independent floor plane detached from the existing building by a two metre interval and also from the rear glass brick wall by a narrow gap. It is a lofty space reached from the old building by a short passageway which bridges the void between old and new. A full width raised roof light accentuates the separation and bathes the reception space in reflected light. A window in the surgery overlooks this area which is more art gallery than traditional dentist's waiting room. Basil Blackshaw's large and epic painting inscribed *The first tractor in Randalstown* dominates one long wall and is faced by a Neil Shawcross but pride of place is reserved for a small William Scott mounted on the end wall.

Simon Templeton has brought his wide experience of gallery design to this project and created a very satisfying fusion of old and new in which one speaks to the other.

DE

Market Place Theatre & Arts Centre

ARMAGH   CO ARMAGH
GLENN HOWELLS ARCHITECTS   2000

Armagh's new theatre is a late flowering of Modernism, in a profoundly historic setting, that engages with its surroundings with suavity and easy assurance. Georgian terraces, on either side of the steeply sloping site, rise towards the high stepped gables and chimneys of the Cathedral Close, behind them the dark mass of St Patrick's Anglican Cathedral crowns the hill. The centrepiece, the former Market House built in 1815 in a solid Palladian style, is perhaps the work of Francis Johnston, a local man who became Architect to the Board of Works and the leading practitioner of his day and who was responsible for a series of notable buildings in Armagh. A third storey was added to the Market

House in 1912 when it became the Technical College. The extension seamlessly continues the ashlar stonework.

The entrance loggia to the theatre, civic in scale, nudges out across the contours at the upper end of Market Place; it is the external expression of the internal concourse which is the interface between the two principal elements of the programme – the theatre and the arts centre. The gallery, studio theatre and studios, on one side, are dug into the hill and on the other the 400 seater auditorium, with its raked floor following the lie of the land. The central concourse is very much the heart and engine room of the plan and if it can be considered a

servant space then it is a very stylish major-domo. It also leads to the walkway that connects with the upper level of the St Patrick's Trian. This cultural centre is entered through the tourist office in English Street, described in the UAHS list as a 'Baroque Revival Mannerist' composition, formerly the Belfast Banking Company and built to designs by Charles Lanyon in 1851. A multi-storey car park occupies the ground between the Trian and the new theatre and serves both buildings. The walkway that connects them links the world of Charles Lanyon with the Modernism of Glenn Howells.

Choice of material is an important consideration when designing a building to

respect its context and here the mixture of Derbyshire limestone and Spanish Dolomite fines, used for the concrete panels, was matched closely with the limestone used in the city. The 350 x 1.200mm cladding panels generate the modular system which applies throughout the building and establishes ceiling heights, floor thicknesses and also the 7.200 x 3.600mm structural grid, visible in the front of house spaces and also in the entrance canopy in Market Place, where circular columns rise through two levels. The use of these polished concrete panels as floors, walls and ceilings as well as externally is a master stroke and highly innovative – it follows the Modernist's mantra 'what you see is what you get'.

There is no interior plaster, suspended ceilings or raised floor. The roof panels 'had to allow indirect lighting into the foyer below and integrate artificial lighting, drainage and services within a shallow depth'. Air conditioning is not used rather, in another innovation, cool air is fed through the hollow cores of the concrete units as a means of evening out the thermal highs and lows.

The theatre abuts the Armagh Film House which occupies a Georgian terraced building and the workshops present a blank wall of precast concrete to Market Place. The scene dock doors are panelled too which makes them almost invisible, a surprising deceit in architecture of such integrity, but

understandable given the civic surroundings. The high loggia set on a plinth with stepped approaches is classic in spirit and civic in scale and makes for that 'engaging ambiguity between inside and outside' that Peter Fawcett has noted. Access to the art gallery is by a lobby with translucent glazing. This double height space reads as a perfect cube with a lowered central ceiling and perimeter glazing. The gallery, studios on two levels, and the studio theatre form three cubic volumes which rise above the roof level of the concourse. The theatre is traditional in layout with a proscenium arch and an orchestra pit; the floor is raked with an under-stage area. The thrust stage can be adjusted to various

0 |_____| 10

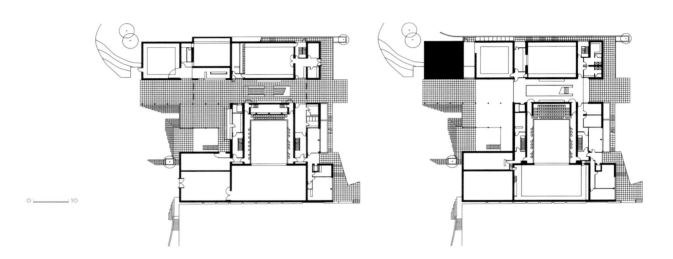

0 |_____| 10

levels for the pit, auditorium and stage to give different performance formats and it can act as a lift for heavy stage equipment. The lofty interior with two gallery levels is lined in American oak with an exposed steelwork lighting grid over. As a means of reducing the height of the conventional fly-tower the architects used a stage loft to house the scenery. The ancillary accommodation, offices and workshops, are arranged about the auditorium and stage, which rise above the roof level of the concourse.

The clarity and pristine organization of the concourse depend upon the discipline applied by the modular wall units and the strips of marginal roof lights, like exposures of a film, that form a luminous edge on each side of the roof slab, lighting the interior and illuminating the side walls. This has the effect of seeming to detach the roof planes from the structure so that they appear as free-floating elements in the manner of de Stijl architecture. This aesthetic movement pioneered an approach to the handling of space where rooms seem to open on all sides and hint at further space beyond, and it is especially evident in the mezzanine foyer, leading to the gallery level of the theatre, where glazed openings separate the floor from the vertical surfaces. There are other precedents too. The sensation of moving between lanes where floor and soffits are alike in grey limestone finish recalls the compressed horizontal spatial flow of Mies van der Röhe's German Pavilion at the World Exhibition, Barcelona, 1929 as does the temple-like entrance with steps approaching a plinth with columns and horizontal roof slab. If this association is perhaps peripheral to the design, the architects do acknowledge a reference to Frank Lloyd Wright's Unity Temple of 1906. The overall massing and the linking of two elements about a central entrance have some striking affinities.

This firm of architects from Birmingham has imported architecture of distinction to the city; the scheme was selected from

References

Arts Council of Northern Ireland. *Building for the arts: celebrating 10 years of Lottery funding.* Belfast, ACNI, 2004. 8-11.

McKinstry, R. et al. *The buildings of Armagh.* Belfast: UAHS, 1992. 112.

Fawcett, P. Master of Arts. *Architects' Journal*, 211(24), 2000. 28-37.

The Market Place Theatre. *UA International*, 16(8), 2000. 28-33.

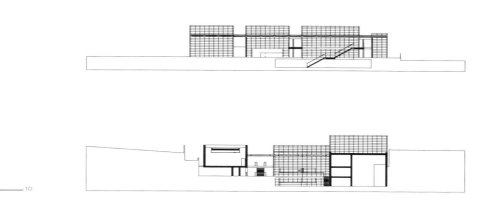

0 ⸺ 10

Evans, D. Civitas.
Perspective, 8(5), 2000. 41-46.

The Market Place Armagh.
Irish Architect, 162, 2000. 27-30.

a field of 76 entries in an international competition. The chief architectural assessor, Richard McCormac, cited it as a design 'of exceptional quality that will work with and readily become part of the social and cultural life of the city'. Ulster architecture has always benefited from the infusion of imported talents. This, too, was a collaborative exercise and the architects have enjoyed the input of local expertise and warmly acknowledge the advice of Robert McKinstry in particular. The building opened in April 2000 and since then its lean and taut presence has become part of the city's life and it belongs to an architectural tradition established in the 18th century, where in the words of the local poet W.R. Rodgers 'reason was all the rage'. It received an RIBA Award in 2000 and the Civic Trust Centre Vision Award in 2001.

DE

Dungloe District Offices

DUNGLOE   CO DONEGAL
MCCULLOUGH MULVIN ARCHITECTS   2002

This project, completed in 2002, was one of a series of decentralised government buildings constructed in Donegal (see also MacGabhann Architects project in Letterkenny, p.140). Designed by different architects but all comparable in scale, each building presented a distinct response to programme and context.

The bog-land site for this building evokes deep archaeological and poetic readings with bog-land having long been considered by some to be both the physical and metaphorical repository of ancient Irish history. In response to this understanding

of the site, the architects have delicately raised the building a few feet above the ground, just sufficiently to detach it so that it lies over rather than on the structurally weak ground. Piled concrete foundations express the need to probe deeply for support and bearing.

As with the building itself, two causeway-like decks are raised slightly above ground, apparently floating, as they stretch across the site with sufficient presence to register as building elements rather than mere landscape surfaces. These explicitly presented routes are, in fact, two ends of

the one element that converge in the foyer space. This space can be best understood as the volume between the building's two primary elements. Of comparable size and proportion, these elements lie side by side with the timber-clad block angled slightly away from the causeway axis towards the south. The other block, aligned with and contiguous to that axis, extends its roof over the foyer to the first block thereby characterizing the foyer as a generous canyon-like space. Perhaps in deference to its detachment from the geometry of the causeway, the southerly block is clad in timber, expressing it as a

References

Civic offices Dungloe, Co Donegal. *Irish Architect*, (172), 2001. 33-37.

Dungloe District Offices, County Donegal. In *Work: McCullough Mulvin Architects*. Dublin; Oysterhaven : Gandon Editions; Anne St Press, 2004. 84-91.

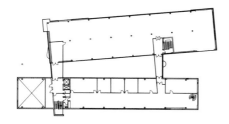
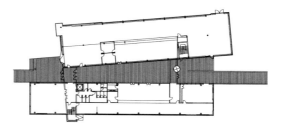

0 ———— 10

0 ———— 10

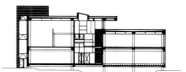

lighter less permanent object dislocated from its heavier rendered neighbour. These two distinct material treatments reflect at once the ancient and the more recent Irish building traditions.

Paradoxically the prevailing impression of this building, despite its humble material qualities and lightness of contact with the ground, is of a rather imposing presence that projects a strongly institutional tone to its distant views. However, the building is accessible, democratic and connected to its community despite appearing as a solitary form evoking lone objects at sea

or on a wind-stripped landscape. And whilst these poetic qualities may not be immediately obvious and are even perhaps overshadowed for most by the building's large scale, the somewhat secret or cryptic nature of its connection with the soft earth below seems appropriately concealed like the dormant traces of history in the bog itself.

AH

Whitehall Square

BELFAST
TODD ARCHITECTS   2001

Sandy Row, Belfast's original road to the south and Dublin, crosses the estuarine sleech of the city centre to join the rising ground of Bradbury Place and the Malone Ridge moving, as Denis Ireland puts it, from slob land to snob land. Whitehall Square occupies this transitional zone on the edge of the plains but it belongs to both worlds. Its main entrance faces the rising ground to the south and the quality and style of the accommodation is that of more fashionable residential areas. Until recent years Sandy Row was a busy thoroughfare lined with shops but today the picture seems to be one of slow decline. The industries of the 19th century, the linen and flax factory, the rope walk, the glue and starch works and the Ulster Brewery, have gone and Murray's Tobacco Factory (which bears the inscription Whitehall Tobacco Works in decorative tiling) has recently closed. This building by Watt &

Tulloch (1900) with its square corner towers and pagoda-like roofs is a strong architectural presence at the Boyne Bridge end of Sandy Row and the Orange Hall, a 'four storey red brick tower like building' is as emphatic at the other end. The Orange Hall, which faces Whitehall Square and Tollgate House, set the precedent for the height of the new building – Sandy Row is predominantly two-storied.

Carvill Group Ltd developed this 0.48 hectare brownfield site as a residential development of some 120 flats with ground floor shopping and car parking on a 1:1 basis. A courtyard at first floor level is enclosed by four blocks of flats presenting brick façades to the outside world which rise to three storeys and four storeys. The fenestration patterns echo those of the red brick terraces of urban Belfast. Above, glazing to the penthouses is set back and

oversailing monopitched roofs rise towards the interior.

The Donegall Road block seems to march to a different tune to the others as it unleashes a geometrical play of cantilevered projections, canted in plan towards the alignment of Donegall Road. At the corner of Sandy Row the penthouse glazing projects beyond the brick façade and descends as an inward tapering, elongated oriel window: a gesture that perhaps belongs to the architecture of Futurism and could be a manifesto for the future of Sandy Row. The dramatic and lofty main entrance beside Malone Place fractures the orthogonal discipline of the plan, imposing upon it sharply triangular forms. To one side of the entrance hall a stuccoed corner thrusts forward to enclose the space and offers a stack of stiletto pointed balconies in galvanized steel and carried by a single

References

Ireland, D. From the jungle of Belfast. In *Footnotes to history, 1904-72*. Belfast, 1973. 40.

Larmour, P. *Belfast: an illustrated architectural guide*. Belfast: Friar's Bush Press, 1987.

Carvill Group scales new heights. *UA International*, 18(8), 2002. 22-31.

McCusker, S. The Apartment. *Perspective*,11(4), 2002. 24-34.

PLAN   0 └─────┘ 10

ELEVATION

SECTION   0 └─────┘ 10

Residential development, Sandy Row, Belfast. *Irish Architect*,180, 2002. 36-37.

Residential development, Sandy Row, Belfast. In Ainley, R (ed). *Architecture 02: The RIBA Awards 84-85*. London: Batsford, 2002.

steel column; on the other the brickwork tapers to a knife edge. The entrance is formed by the gap between the blocks and the treatment refers to the pattern of urban Belfast where terraces generally do not turn the corner but end abruptly at a gable and resume at right angles to leave an interval between them. A straight flight of stairs leads to the first floor courtyard – an enclave of continental urbanity and sophistication, trapezoidal in plan and flaring out towards the south. The floorscape is paved and pebbled. Trees with spherical tops borrowed, as it were, from the perspective drawings of Charles Rennie Mackintosh, punctuate the space and an elongated narrow pool, meridian-like, runs longitudinally from north to south. Rendered walls and balconies overlook this recreational and meeting space and the glazed penthouses, with double height volumes are inclined inwards from the façades.

The two main entrances, both on Sandy Row, give access to the courtyard from where the generous provision of six sets of stairs and lifts, with a good range of modern painting, ensures that the internal corridors to the flats are relatively short as well as ample in width – a lesson drawn from the architect's continental experience. The retail units are situated beneath the flats on the Donegall Road and the Sandy Row frontages and are serviced from the car park area which occupies the remainder of the ground floor and is reached by Blondin Street at the rear of the site. The height of the car park was determined by the retail units and it was sufficient to allow a downward projection of one metre from the planting bed for the ornamental trees which rise from courtyard level.

The Sandy Row residents' forum warmly welcomed this major development when it was first proposed. It would have a regenerating effect upon this inner city area which, it was felt, had been largely ignored and deprived of major investment. To what extent these hopes have been realised it is perhaps too early to judge but the failure to let any of the ground floor retail units on Sandy Row and Donegall Road has not helped matters. The flats, despite some difficulties, have proved very successful and this project must surely represent a first step in the renaissance of Sandy Row and the public perception of the area.

DE

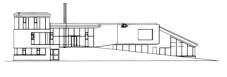

WEST ELEVATION

Letterkenny Council Offices

LETTERKENNY CO DONEGAL
MACGABHANN ARCHITECTS   2002

Located in Ireland's most north-westerly county, this building addresses the problem of designing good architecture in the context of the often featureless urban periphery. The arrangement of car park and warehouse, so typical of drive-by commercial suburbs everywhere, is understood but also questioned. The architect acknowledges the absence of a conventional urban or rural context and looks to more abstract or thematic devices to ensure this building makes connections with its site.

The architect in designing this building makes reference to the autonomous architecture of the retail shed and also draws heavily on the theme of landscape

to ensure that the building is integrated with its site. The understanding of landscape here eschews the romantic pastoral view, instead recognising as equally significant both the hard man-made presence of the ring road and car parks and the surrounding agricultural landscape peppered with nondescript bungalows. The building mediates between these two contexts. To the town, it presents itself as an inclined concrete plane (the car park) which eventually returns, or folds back on itself, to project a façade which makes the building appear to look over its shoulder to the distant presence of the cathedral. To the countryside, it is the prevailing presence of the unifying sedum-grassed

roof plane (again cranked and distorted to accommodate the internal volumes) that makes the connection; this abstract representation of field or hillside is punctured by lanterns that seem peeled out of the surface to transmit daylight to the deep plan underneath. Curtain walling connects the edges of the roof plane to the lower levels and eventually carries on down to the ground thus ensuring that the roof is defined as a plane or an artificial landscape.

The programme for the project, which is essentially a decentralized government office, is interpreted by the architect as an extension of the external car park surface

References

Ryan, R. Letterkenny Area Office (LAO) for Donegal. *Irish Architect*, 179, 2002. 15-19, 47.

O'Toole, S. In the ascendant. *Sunday Times* (London), 4 August 2002.

Black, S. Town and Country Club. *RIBA Journal*,109 (9), 2002. 34-40.

SECTIONS

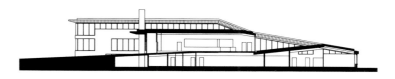

0 ————— 10

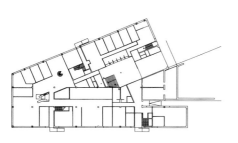

GROUND FLOOR

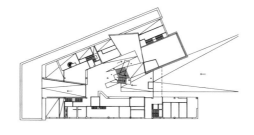

FIRST FLOOR

SECOND FLOOR

0 ——— 10

into the building as a continuous concrete plate that folds and realigns as it defines the internal public concourse and foyers, allowing visitors to interact within a relaxed artificial landscape in an informal way whilst going about the formalities of their visit. The floor terminates at its highest level in the Council Chamber itself which, as a democratic gesture, is characterized as an extension of the foyer with a vast pivoting door opening up the whole room and, symbolically, its purpose for public involvement. The timber lining to this space distinguishes it from the rest of the foyer. Appropriately, the chamber window looks toward the town projecting a civic quality as it cantilevers out over the car park.

The sense of continuously flowing space is reasserted through ingenious detail flanking the edges of the internal floor-plate. Whilst initially functioning as a handrail, this amalgam of metalwork and joinery adjusts in scale and proportion to create high level benches (where visitors can complete paperwork) as well as low-level seating. The prevalence of this ever-adjusting detail unifies the interior foyers underneath the concrete soffit of the roof plan - the informal deployment of both roof lights and light fittings in this surface reflects the relaxed circulation below.

Radical yet civic, informal but spatially direct, this project revels in its paradoxical qualities. Although rooted in a central European building culture (as exemplified by Daniel Libeskind, Rem Koolhaas and others) and despite its unfamiliar geometries, this building makes an appropriately understated addition to this remote corner of the continent.

AH

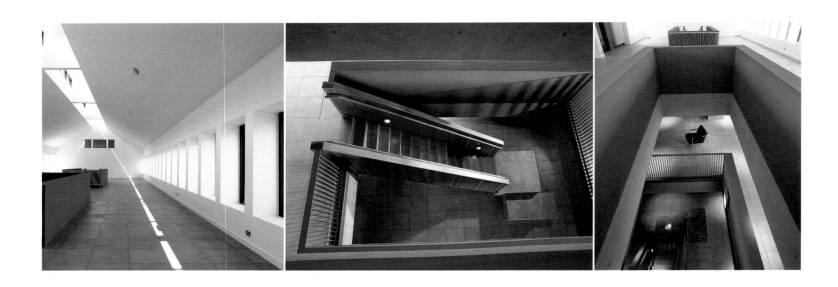

Batik Showrooms & Offices

BELFAST
TWENTY TWO OVER SEVEN   2005

That gasworks could aspire to civic pretension might seem unlikely; historically they gravitated towards the industrial fringes of cities. The Dubliners' ballad 'Dirty Old Town' opens with the evocative line 'I met my love by the gasworks wall' but here in Belfast, it seems, we did things differently. Our gasworks wall is a fine example of civic architecture of the late Victorian period. The long range of offices in red brick with terracotta panels, which forms part of the Ormeau Road frontage includes a circular clock tower, and the massive Klondyke Building presents a giant pediment in brickwork with the arms of Belfast carved in sandstone. These buildings, the arcaded brick wall which links them and the Meter House in the

heart of the site, are the only survivors of the industry which closed in 1985. The giant gasholder, a major Belfast landmark, and the various structures associated with the industry, have now gone, leaving some 11 hectares of building land and a site of enormous potential to the regeneration of Belfast. It also raised the question of what should be the appropriate response to building on this almost blank canvas, once the ground had been decontaminated. Should the architecture engage in some sort of dialogue with the character of the Linen Quarter nearby, reflect something of the site's history or forge a new vision for the future of the city? The development of the site as a 'business park' is now proceeding, but as yet no clear

or unified vision has emerged for the design of new buildings. The Halifax Building is a ghost-like reminder of the gasholder both in its size and its siting beside the Lagan.

Twenty two over seven is building on two sites to either side of the entrance which faces Donegall Pass and features two ornamental brick sculptures in the form of miniature factory chimneys. The Batik showrooms and office building to the right of the entrance shows an individual and personal response to the context. It is a linear development of two three-storey blocks linked and connecting with the Meter House that steps up in height towards the Ormeau Road. The lower floors are reinforced concrete frames and

the roof is steel portals. Terne-coated steel is used as a roof finish, as cladding to the links and on the second floor showrooms where the longitudinal roof light makes for a distinctive gable on the Ormeau Road frontage. The terne-coated steel has now lost its shimmering appearance and weathered to a sober and dignified grey. The external walls are white render with timber spandrels between the ground and first floor windows to emphasize the columnar structure. Cills and plinths are in grey granite.

There is a touch of the puritan about the interior which makes a vibrant setting for the display of high quality furniture; the high cill levels convey something of the

Victorian classroom and high moral purpose. Concrete beams and soffits are painted white and the floors are grey porcelain tiles. The stairs are terse and economic, straight flights with solid timber balustrades rise from polished concrete plinth blocks in the centre of the plan. The second floor is a tent-like experience, the inclined roof planes are undifferentiated from the walls and the clerestory bathes the interior in suffused lighting. At around noon, on a fine day, a gleam of sunlight slices along the interior. Service elements, fire escapes and lifts are housed beside the link between the blocks and also in a small ancillary wing which projects on the south side to enclose a tiny courtyard beside the boundary wall.

The architects expressed the design intention of associating this building with the urbanism of the Linen Quarter nearby, the double height concrete columns elevate the scale to civic dimension and another reference point was the work of the Scots architect Alexander 'Greek' Thomson who was instrumental in creating the urban imagery of Glasgow. His strong vertical emphasis and long horizontal lines of fenestration with dense metronomic rhythms are evident here. The use of terne-coated steel, it was felt, had appropriate industrial connotations and another instance of keeping Ruskin's Lamp of Memory alight (a gas lamp?) is the distinctive gable form. In *An introduction to modern Ulster architecture,*

an illustration shows a similar gable projecting from the brick structures which once towered above the boundary wall. Today the eye is drawn towards the Batik building which despite its modest size, possesses a sense of the monumental which relates to the Klondyke Building at the end of the site. As noted in *Perspective*, 'it could also be read as a metaphor of a much smaller object: a reliquary or shrine for holy relics, which in Ireland were wooden boxes, shaped like a house or a church and clad in metal plates'.

Further buildings, now on site, include an office block running parallel to the former offices of the Gasworks and using much the same handling as the Batik building. At the Cromac Street approach the plan tapers to a flat-iron-like profile with bull-nose point, performing, as it were, a duet with the corner of the former gas offices nearby. A second new office block, situated to the rear is severe and measured in expression – an essay in the art of 'brickmanship' that belongs to the factory buildings of our industrial heritage. These unfinished buildings, it seems, will maintain the themes of memory and context already established in the Batik building which is architecture of deep conviction, rooted in its context and the recipient of an RIBA Award in 2002.

References

Ruskin, J. *The seven lamps of architecture*. London: New York: JM Dent: EP Dutton, 1907.

Evans, D. *An introduction to modern Ulster architecture*. Belfast: UAHS, 1977. 31.

Evans, D. Northern fusions. *Perspective*, 12(4), 2003. 22-30.

Brett, CEB. *Buildings of Belfast 1700-1914*. Rev. ed. Belfast: Friar's Bush Press, 1985.

NORTH ELEVATION

SECTION

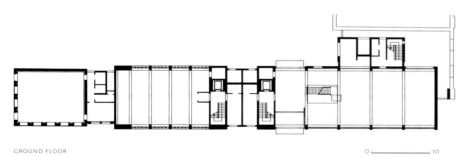

GROUND FLOOR

0 ⌐_____⌐ 10

The Potthouse

BELFAST
BOX ARCHITECTS LTD   2003–4

Bold in its massing and clear cut in its definition of form, the building has an appropriate downtown big city feel, without a hint of conservation area caution in its design. It is the kind of architecture that brings traditionalists out in protest and Modernists reaching for superlatives. Waring Street is at the heart of the old town of Belfast; it is shown on Thomas Phillips's map of 1685, and the past was a major influence on the design of this building which can be likened to a palimpsest – a parchment written on twice, where traces of the original show through.

The name comes from the pothouse which occupied the site in the late 17th century. It produced Delftware which was exported all over Europe and was the largest pottery in the British Isles. A recent archaeological excavation uncovered many artefacts relating to the industry and it also revealed foundations and masonry walls of a terrace of houses, believed to be the first to be built in Belfast, which housed the pothouse workers and faced on to Waring Street. This vestigial structure established the grid of the three-storey high range of box-like 'snugs' that characterize the main façade. Their form, too, is important in the spatial organization of the scheme. The building's footprint is 20 x 20 metres and at 19 metres in height it is almost a cube – the top floor of continuously glazed office space was a late addition to the brief and its impact upon the overall form is

not strong. The form is articulated as three spatial entities. An inverted L takes up the two-storied offices, with their casually sporadic fenestration, and the service spaces, stairs, lifts, bars and toilets to the rear. This form, introverted and solid, is supported at the Waring Street front by the box-frames of the fully glazed snugs. The enclosed volume behind includes the ground floor Potthouse bar and grill, the first floor Sugar Room nightclub and the second floor Soap Bar Guest Room – further references to the site's industrial heritage. These spaces are given external expression by the storey-height Reglit glazing which is suffused in a yellow glow by night. The full drama of these spaces is only revealed on entry. A canyon of glass-

References

Clarke, P. Time lines. *Perspective*, 14 (7), 2005. 16-25.

Kucharek, J. Potted history. *Interiors for Architects and Designers*, (30),2005. 39-42.

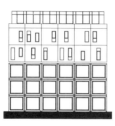

ELEVATIONS   SECTION

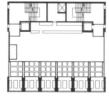

GROUND FLOOR   FIRST FLOOR   FOURTH FLOOR   0 ————— 10

floored space carves through the interior from the Hill Street side to Cotton Court; the disco floors resemble trays overlooking the void which also separates the three-storey range of snugs which recapitulate the form of the original 17th century terrace as a seemingly free-standing structure.

The vertigo-inducing void is framed in exposed steelwork, painted dark grey, which establishes the raw industrial flavour of the interior, services are surface mounted and the floors are polished concrete. The tables, in concrete, snake around the steel columns like a 'conga' at a party; a layout so disjointed and fragmentary as to suggest something of the relics of broken pottery which were discovered during the

excavation of the site, and one designed to encourage informality and cross table conversation between diners. The oak chairs, designed by the architects, are three-legged to provide maximum stability. The open cubes on Waring Street are reworkings, complete with fireplaces, of the traditional snug, the Irishman's retreat from the world but here they are wide open to it. Seen from inside or out the clientele appears like actors in a play, such is the effect of the picture-frame-like surround to each opening.

Cathedral Quarter has been for some time on the verge of realizing its ambition to become a focal point for Belfast's art and culture in much the same way as the

Temple Bar area has for Dublin. This exuberant contribution to the nightlife of the area, which won an RIBA Award in 2005, should move things along very nicely.

DE

Carton Le Vert House & Studio

RATHMULLAN   CO DONEGAL
MACGABHANN ARCHITECTS   2003–5

SECTIONS   0 |————————| 10

The work of this practice can be seen to question the conventions of architectural form and representation rarely deviated from in Ulster. This project, whilst modest in scale, creates a radical form in the landscape yet has its roots firmly anchored in the pragmatic building tradition of north-west Ulster.

The plan is divided into two clear elements. The first, with its narrow wedge-shaped footprint, contains the service elements of the building programme – kitchen, bathroom, entrance; the second, a longer rectilinear element, accommodates the living spaces and bedrooms.

The material used in the two pieces distinguishes them – the smaller wedge block being constructed from in situ concrete marked with boards similar to those used to clad the external skin of the larger block in order to express a lighter sense of construction. The clear internal distinction between the two elements enriches the experience of the house and works with its small scale – as one passes between the two zones, the articulation of the junction seems to indicate other possibilities of what might have been. It is as though there are two tiny houses which, together, feel more generous than one single house of the same area.

The material of the two roof forms gives external expression to the two plan elements – slate tiles over the concrete wedge and corrugated metal over the lighter timber element. Despite this, the external distinction of the two pieces is somewhat ambiguous – the house reads more clearly as one timber-faceted container. However, further cohesion of this form will occur as the timber cladding slowly mellows in colour to silvery grey leaving little visual distinction between wood and concrete.

To the west of the house sits a small studio block clad with corrugated metal

References

Carton Le Vert House, Rathmullan, Co Donegal. *Architecture Ireland*, (191), 2003. 44-45.

Ferienhaus in Donegal: holiday home in Donegal. *AW Architektur & Wettbewerbe*, (199), 2004. 30-31.

Green Box Design Studio, Rathmullan, Co Donegal. *Architecture Ireland*, (210), 2005. 54-55.

0 ‖—————————— 10

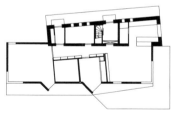

GROUND FLOOR

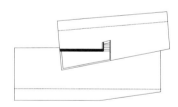

ROOF & FIRST FLOOR

evoking the character of vernacular rural outbuildings. The prevalence of timber over metal in the house is inverted here – in the studio, timber is not used for cladding but rather for the detail of the window frames. The long, striated nature of the windows speaks of connections with the panoramic views over the countryside whilst the western wall tips gently away from the roof at the studio's south-west corner to draw the evening sun across the angled ceiling plane.

These two little buildings feel like good neighbours, old friends even – different, sure enough of their own personalities, but

charged with the same sense of a simple, raw quality that resists any concessions to conventional ideas of architectural beauty.

AH

Office Building, Linenhall Street

BELFAST
BUILDING DESIGN PARTNERSHIP   2004

Belfast's city centre has been marred in the latter years of the 20th century by developer-driven, superficial architecture that detracts from the dignity of the late Victorian warehouses that once predominated in the area south of the City Hall.

By contrast, this office building delivers more than mere lettable square-footage – it understands its place in the urban fabric and connects to the city by responding to the scale and gravitas of its location opposite the rear portico of the City Hall. The unadorned precision of its stone and glass skin and the confident detailing and proportions that transcend architectural

fashion give the building a quiet dignity. Presented as carefully considered skins of Portland stone and glass stretched tautly over the structural frame, the main façades of the building appear weighty and robust although, on closer inspection, the delicacy and dignified refinement of the construction becomes apparent.

The top-most levels (stepped back terrace-like in section) seem less assured. Enclosed in curtain-walling rimmed with brise-soleil, these floors are a somewhat incidental and flimsy addition to the otherwise convincing lower mass. Curved on plan (a gesture to Donegall Square West) and

with a deeper terrace, the top floor seems unnecessarily at odds with the prevailing orthogonal character of the primary stone-clad grid.

The building is particularly interesting in that it appears reassuringly solid on the exterior whilst delivering a luminous and almost ethereal quality within. At ground and first floor level the façade recesses from the street to establish a careful disconnection from the pavement. The column members of the grid drop past the double-height space to form a tall colonnade around the corner – a generous gesture to the city allowing for

References

Gallagher, S. 6-9 Donegall Square South. *Perspective*,13 (3), 2004. 50-56.

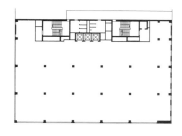

SECOND · FIFTH FLOORS

GROUND FLOOR   0 ——— 10

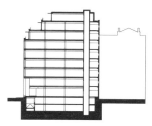

SECTION

SIDE ELEVATION   0 ——— 10

some mediation between street and interior. The understated good judgement extends into the building where the clean alignment on plan of all services and cores to the party wall leaves the three façades free to address the city. Whilst the north and west façades are characterized predominantly by the colonnade, the south façade's proportion of glazing-to-stone-cladding is adjusted to read as an array of tall windows – a more appropriate language for the narrow side street.

The office floors open up expansively to full-height glazing, the unobtrusive detailing of which results in the façades of

the neighbouring buildings giving visual definition to the edges of the office areas. This gives the interiors a feeling of spaciousness that is unexpected in such a dense urban area. Although the fenestration is measured out in bays between columns, there are panoramic views of the city – strangely abstracted because of the height above street level of the upper floors and the absence of traffic noise. Views to the back of the City Hall reinvigorate the reading of the older building – inviting us to look again.

This is a building that asserts Belfast's city credentials – its urbane tones lend it

a sense of longevity. It is here to stay. The severity of the Portland stone grid engages with both the neo-Classical City Hall and with the contemporary buildings nearby, most notably the Northern Bank building of 1977 in Donegall Square West also designed by Building Design Partnership.

AH

Bunscoil an tSléibhe Dhuibh

BELFAST
MACKEL & DOHERTY   2005

Schools, having in earlier years been a building type known for architectural experimentation and excellence (see Kennedy FitzGerald & Associates' Glenveagh School, p.108), have suffered over recent years as a result of low professional fees and construction budgets which have made conditions difficult for architects who want to create stimulating environments for the education of future generations. Despite such unhelpful conditions, and perhaps all the more significantly, a few projects have emerged in recent years that have managed to produce creative designs even under such constraints.

This project for a seven-classroom primary school was built in a disadvantaged area of west Belfast in 2004. Strict design guidelines have been deftly reinterpreted to obviate the need for corridor-like spaces. Instead, the whole plan is organised around the glazed courtyard as a series of concentric zones: the outermost being the school grounds, next the classrooms and then the informal teaching space around the courtyard's timber-framed enclosure. This apparently overtly internalised gesture could be read negatively insofar as it cuts the school off from its neighbourhood, yet it makes sense against an appreciation of the peripheral landscape around the site where a collection of unremarkable, even ill-designed, buildings define the area's tough urban qualities. The courtyard offers an alternative environment with its secure and peaceful enclosure which is used as an informal teaching space or play area, providing a controlled environment that juxtaposes strongly with the visual 'looseness' of the surrounding neighbourhood.

All classrooms have an external glazed connection to the main site – and so, in a sense, they operate as connecting space

References

Gallagher, S. A different school of thought. *Perspective*,14(3), 2005. 30-36.

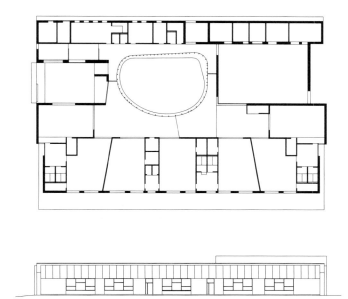
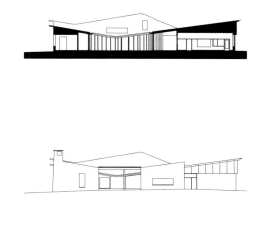

0 |_____| 10

between the city and the courtyard – a radical reallocation of apparent function given the traditional model of internal corridor with classroom-space to either side. This enriches the experience of the classroom raising its character above static enclosure to a space offering stimulation and opportunities for teaching. Paradoxically, it is from within the courtyard that the presence of the distant hilltop of Black Mountain can be registered most clearly as it appears above the profile of the curving eaves. The sense of simple space connecting with distant countryside (a recurrent quality of Belfast

as a city set within its mountain rim) is a small revelation.

The main external form of the school is fragmented to create a sense of collected pieces that mediate between the large size of the building and the need to engage with the young pupils. External timber cladding and some coloured walls all contribute to an informal environment largely free of institutional references.

The fact this project was achieved under the tight budget typical of the education sector is worthy of note but even more

important is the fact that it is evidence of the ability of architects to find solutions that can transform the experience of day-to-day activities from the mundane to the exceptional even in unpromising circumstances.

AH

Stepping House

ARÁINN MHÔR ISLAND   CO DONEGAL
LiD ARCHITECTURE: DOUGAL SHERIDAN, DEIRDRE MCMENAMIN   2005

Sited on an island off the western coast of Co Donegal, this small house feels as though it is caught somewhere between the influence of the vernacular and a desire to harmonise with the tough landscape peppered with wind-stripped rock outcrops in which it is sited. Where other comparably sized homes on the island take the simple pitched-roof form as their parti, this house takes its inspiration from the rugged terrain that seems forever unwelcoming to any gesture of habitation. The angular forms of the house allude to those of a great boulder, chipped and eroded but finally settled into the landscape as though tumbled down to its final site.

The internal arrangement of the house can also be understood in terms of landscape and topography – a series of internal terraces, duplicating the incline of the hillside on which the house sits, is the dominating organisational device. To make your way from bed to breakfast table is to go down the hill whilst the split level around the seating area imitates the rocky outcrop nearby. The artificial or constructed landscape is a theme in contemporary architecture that runs through the work of other Irish practices such as MacGabhann Architects (see p.140). What is interesting here is the immediacy of the relationship of the house to the untouched ground around it – an abrupt quality that seems appropriately direct for this place where precision and beauty of finish must give way to a pragmatic robustness. Whilst two terraces sit sheltered within the mass

References

Clark, K. Landscape into art. London: J. Murray, 1976.

Mackel, C. Stepping house, Arainn Mhor. Perspective,14(5), 2005. 46-53.

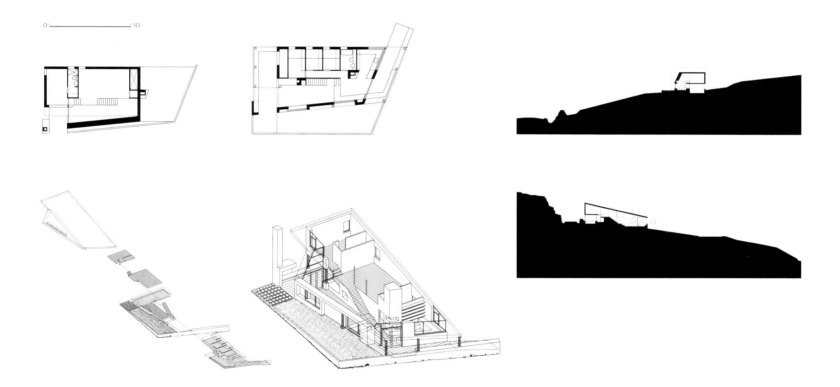

of the main building, only a single grassed terrace, elevated a few feet above the wild terrain, extends outward to engage the landscape proper.

Despite its small area this house has a generous feel achieved by the loose definition of the internal-to-external areas. In one sense the horizon defines the edge of the occupants' world when sitting in the sheltered outdoor terrace with the fireplace and the uppermost bedroom overhanging above. In other areas, however, the house feels snugger and internalised giving a sense of protection underneath the sculpted internal form of the roof. Externally, the roof is lined with corrugated fibre-cement sheets – a material more usually associated with low-key agricultural buildings.

There is an undertone of deference to, and acceptance or even respect of, the physical severity of the island, which sits on the very edge of Europe, braced against the Atlantic. Rather than presenting a picturesque ideal of beauty, there is a kind of poetic crudeness to this house. To quote Kenneth Clark, one of the architect's own favourite references for the project: 'Nature... is still disturbing, vast and fearful; and lays open the mind to many dangerous thoughts'.

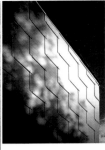

Architect's Own House

RANDALSTOWN   CO ANTRIM
ALAN JONES ARCHITECTS   2005

This house, designed by the architect for himself and his family, occupies a deep but elevated plot sited adjacent to a 19th-century Presbyterian church in a small rural town. Like the church, the house is treated as a single independent structure with its traditional and familiar pitched form taking on an abstract quality by enlarging its dimensions to the boundary of domestic scale. This abstract quality is further developed by the use of dark fibre-cement slate as the external skin to both the roof and the walls giving continuity through the material that extends over almost all of the building.

The simple, almost primitive, form is treated as an empty shell or container with the basement, ground floor and walls constructed from concrete cast in situ. The concrete is finished in two different methods. On the walls it has been cast within coarse particleboard shutters to deliver strongly textured surfaces that catch light dropping down from small roof lights and triangulated cuts in the floor above. The ground floor, in contrast to the textured walls, is finished to a smooth surface dyed to a mid-grey tone. This finish is used throughout the entire ground floor as a unifying feature.

The internal walls and upper floor are constructed from lightweight timber and plasterboard distinguishing them from the heavy concrete shell of the primary volume.

These lighter elements are allowed to detach and deviate from the concrete structure creating angular cuts and geometries that further express the two modes of construction.

The house is approached from the north-east where a single tall, slotted window gives the only expression to an otherwise blank gable. The basement garage is located underneath this gable and visitors gain access to the house via one of two portals cut into the north-west flank of the house and indicated by lightweight canopies. The first of these operates more as a front door whilst the second, closer to the rear and adjacent to the kitchen, is used on a more day-to-day basis. Except in terms of proximity to the road, however, there is

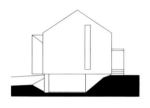

ELEVATIONS

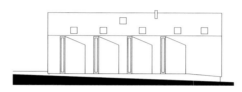

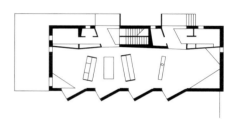

SECTIONS

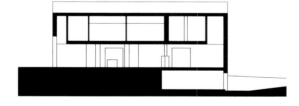

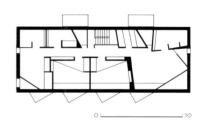

0 |_____| 10

no real distinction between the two doors – this reinforces the idea of the ground floor as one continuous space with the ambiguous nature of the dual hallways having an informal quality that will allow the interior spaces to be more interchangeable in their function. The two hallways are cut through a zone of the plan – a strip that runs the length of the house and contains the secondary accommodation and the stair. This device gives a sense of transition when moving through into the vast ground floor space; the hallways can be closed off by means of large sliding doors.

The far side of the house gathers south light into the ground floor space by means of four splayed bays that provide views

down over a stream and across into the churchyard. The kitchen is designed as a series of elements loosely laid in to the ground floor space as three islands inviting an informal and varied pattern of occupation. The upper floor is more conventional relying heavily upon roof lights for daylight and ventilation. The overhead light drops down over both hallways.

Despite its large mass there is a surprising sense of modesty about the project as it strives towards a kind of 'matter-of-factness'. As with much contemporary Swiss architecture, by which the architect is inspired, the essence of this project lies somewhere between its abstraction and its ordinariness as it demonstrates that a

house can be the embodiment of a strong architectural idea in a culture more often preoccupied with luxury and expressions of personal status.

AH

Falls Leisure Centre

BELFAST
KENNEDY FITZGERALD & ASSOCIATES   2005

The sharp crystalline qualities of this building on the Falls Road set it apart from much of Belfast's predominantly brick and masonry architecture. The milky colours of the translucent glass skin echo the muted tones of the typically overcast skies above the building whilst its robust orthogonal mass alludes to the simple but purposeful forms of Belfast's shipyards and disused linen mills.

The fundamental characteristics of this building are its visual permeability and interconnectedness that allow the various activities within to affect the overall experience of the building beyond each allocated space. This quality, achieved

through layers of glass screens, gives the building a feeling of generosity that belies its compact planning within a small compressed site. This sense of the building being revealed gives the visitor an unusually privileged and intimate contact with it that begins on the pavement where controlled views through clear glazing (contrasting with the surrounding translucent panels) present the building's internal theatre. A long horizontal window to the primary elevation allows the pool hall to engage with the street – the view in to this 'other world' is juxtaposed with the familiarity of the passing traffic. High on the side elevation the long plan form of the gym breaks through the building envelope

as a huge glazed aperture addressing long views over the city.

In contrast to the clear glass, the dominating external glazing is translucent. Formed from double-glazing units of coloured glass with diffusing intermediate layers, these units soften and transmit daylight into the building, permeating the interior with a luminous and even quality of light reminiscent of the façade's persistently neutral tones. Roof lights allow more direct sunlight, controlled through deep louvres, into the primary spaces of the sports hall, where the louvres are particularly noticeable, and also into the pool hall. After daylight hours the building's character is

References

Hall, A. In at the deep end. *Perspective*, 14(4), 2005. 22-29.

Falling for Falls. *Ulster Architect*, 21(5), 2005, 24-25, 27-28.

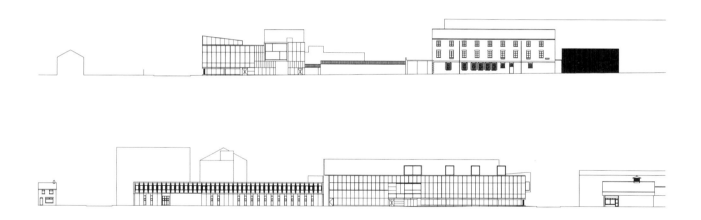

radically transformed as light is transmitted from the building itself through the coloured glass to the street where the building appears as a kind of lantern – a wonderful object in an otherwise unbeautiful place.

Much of Kennedy FitzGerald's earlier work is characterized by powerful sectional relationships between internal volumes (see Portadown Technical College p.88) and the Falls Road Leisure Centre further explores this. The longitudinal section is particularly powerful in that the primary volumes of both the pool hall and the sports hall can be visually 'possessed' from the central foyer areas. This relationship is particularly immediate given the compact

nature of the building and the vertical depth of the sports hall which is cut one storey below ground level. The main staircase is set in the centre of the plan and is detailed as a distinct architectural element around which the plan can be seen to radiate loosely. The staircase and its associated upper and lower foyers feel continually connected to the building's primary spaces beyond.

In a local building culture more character-ized by its insular qualities, this building is significant in that it draws from a central European sensibility where more abstract architectural values predominate. Its tough spatial robustness speaks of an

architecture with real social and regenerative purpose that reasserts the power of section as fundamental to architectural design – a concept somewhat undervalued in Ulster over recent decades. Against a climate of diluted Modernism, the delicate painterly qualities of the façades reassert the role of an architect's intuition – a building's character is more than a product of function.

AH

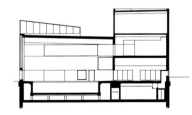
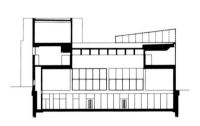

0 |_____| 10

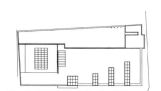
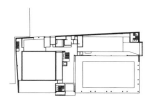

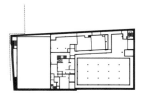

0 ⊢——— 10

NI Railways Train Care Centre

BELFAST
ROBINSON PATTERSON PARTNERSHIP   2002–5

This elegant and highly visible structure is a declaration of a progressive future for rail travel in Northern Ireland. The sleek and visually seamless fuselage, some 170 metres in length, runs parallel to the M2 at the approach to Belfast and 'it is a state-of-the-art facility for the cleaning and maintenance of the 23 new C3K trains, delivered to Northern Ireland Railways in 2005.' It is both sophisticated and industrial in appearance and by night, when floodlit and when the illuminated interior is glimpsed by the passing motorist, it can evoke something of the drama and excitement of the Futurists' vision of speed and industrialised travel. The elegance

and panache of the structure reflects the presence of Ove Arup and Partners as project managers – an internationally renowned firm of consultant engineers whose portfolio of major projects, which includes Sydney Opera House, reads like a Golden Treasury of Modernism.

Roof and walls form a single curvilinear canopy in ribbed aluminium, with integrated roof lights, which is carried on a series of steel portal frames. These spring from a raised edge beam in reinforced concrete which lifts the shell a metre above ground level. A large full height window interrupts the motorway façade, cutting vertically

through the shell to give motorists a sight of the interior working. The junction between the aluminium and the edge beam, which is faced in brickwork, is handled with finesse; a thin louvred strip, which provided natural ventilation, separates the shell and the plinth to give a crisp definition to the two elements. Rainwater discharges into a perimeter land drain.

The end elevations reveal the crab shell profile of the long interior volume. Staff enter through the north gable where a full height glazed lobby leads to toilet and changing rooms at ground level with staff and drivers' accommodation above. On

References

Cowser, A. All aboard. *Perspective*, 15(3). 2006. 76-82

SECTION

ELEVATIONS

ROOF PLAN

FLOOR PLAN

0 —— 10

the south side five train lines enter and by stacking up, line astern, ten trains can be serviced at any given time. The handling of both end façades is workmanlike and form is a direct expression of interior function.

The railways have seen leaner times since their heyday in Victorian times and in the first phase of the Industrial Revolution. Great city terminals like Lime Street Liverpool and St Pancras London acted as spectacular gateway buildings but they masked the train sheds behind. These cast iron, steel and glass structures are hailed as the cathedrals of the 19th century. The terminals projected a powerful image

through their architecture and were highly functional thanks to their engineering but there was little integration between the two. This new building for Northern Ireland Railways, however, is a positive fusion of image and technology.

DE

PART THREE

PROJECTS

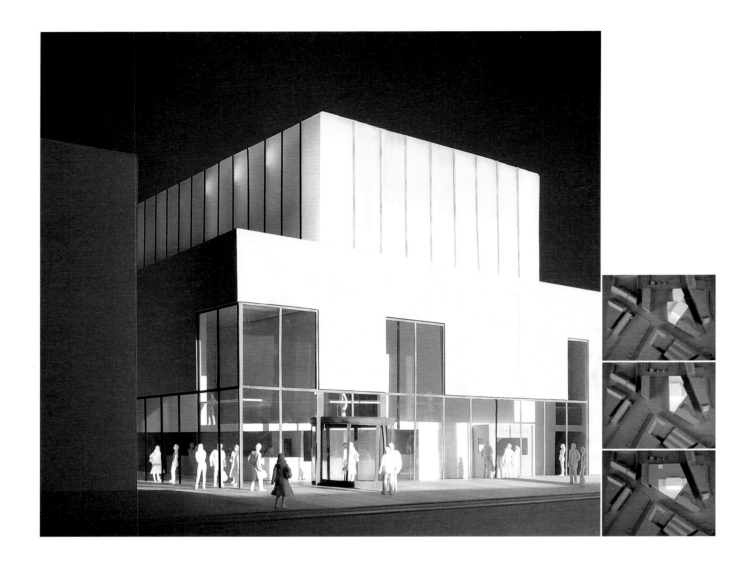

Arts, Cultural & Exhibition Centre

STRABANE   CO LONDONDERRY
ALAN JONES ARCHITECTS & GLENN HOWELLS ARCHITECTS   2005

This project, due for completion in 2006, was a competition winner in 2003 and represents a key element in Strabane's programme of urban regeneration through culture and the arts. The location was selected with the intention of restoring to this area of the town something of its community flavour. At one time it possessed a busy commercial life; the new theatre overlooks the former canal basin, now filled in to form an amenity area – a generous space framed by rendered terracing and known as 'The Score'. The Butter and Pork Market overlooked the basin in historic times but it, too, has gone and it provides the site for the new theatre. A pedestrian route links The Score to Railway

Street in the hinterland of the town; it forms one edge of the triangular site which the theatre shares with the new library.

The theatre occupies the base of the triangle, facing the pedestrian route with the library at the apex. The 256-seater auditorium backs against the library building and the foyer spaces at the perimeter of the plan overlook Railway Street and the pedestrian area. The auditorium is multi-purpose. Retractable bleacher seating and an adjustable orchestra pit mean that the entire auditorium, including the stage area, can provide an uninterrupted floor space capable of housing major exhibitions, including motor shows as vehicles can

enter backstage from Canal Street. The traditional theatre format can also be adapted for concert performances to include choir seating at the back of the stage. The theatre is ringed on three sides by a narrow balcony, and the massive cavity walling houses the air handling ducts. The lofty interior includes a stage fly-tower and a lighting grid housed in the deep trusses. The front of house space rises to a triple height in a narrow strip along the main frontages and the first floor gallery and foyer overlooks this space which acts as a threshold between inside and outside. The external stone paving carries through into this area to meet the wood-strip flooring used inside the foyers and

References

O'Kane, M. Regeneration. *Perspective*,13(6), 2004. 38-46.

Arts Council of Northern Ireland. *Building for the arts: celebrating 10 years of Lottery funding.* Belfast, ACNI, 2004. 8-11.

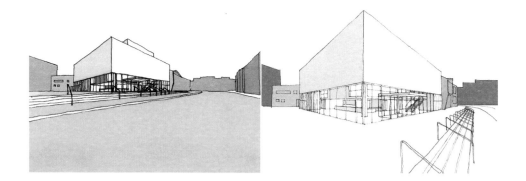
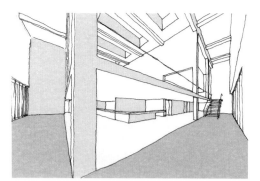

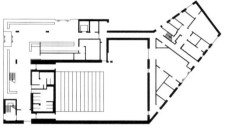

0 ——— 10   GROUND FLOOR

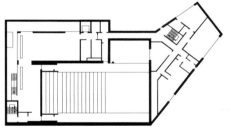

FIRST FLOOR

auditorium. The foyer glazing is no more than 'shop-front' in height. Above, a textured and rendered finish differentiates it from the smooth rendering of the adjacent library. The auditorium is clad in metal sheeting.

Alan Jones hopes that in future this building will assume something of the role and status that the town halls of the 19th century once enjoyed; buildings in the heart of towns that were places for meeting and socializing as well as venues for drama and music.

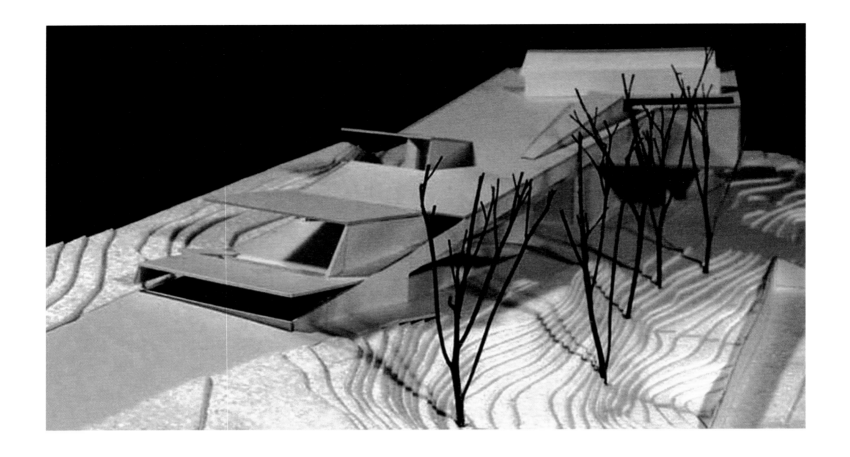

Letterkenny Arts Centre

LETTERKENNY   CO DONEGAL
MACGABHANN ARCHITECTS   2005

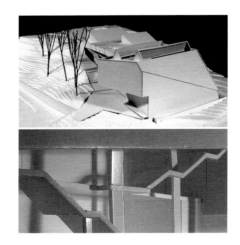

This project, which commenced on site in 2005, continues MacGabhann Architects' exploration of radical architectural forms that, whilst growing naturally out of the demands of the site and programme, both confront and question their physical surroundings.

Despite containing a variety of distinct functions and large volumes, this building expresses itself as a single-faceted metallic form with long wedge-like proportions. Roof lights grow out of the primary mass as secondary elements inserted or folded out of its surface. Further to these minor articulations, the major upper level gallery space is extended out towards the

main approach, thereby hinting at its sectional form and addressing the town as a blank cantilevered gable clad with large aluminium shingles. As is the pattern with this building type, a 'black-box' multi-function space is included – here it is neatly and appropriately tucked into the building's lowest area underneath the main gallery. A ramp provides access to this lower level from the main foyer and mirrors the external topography of the hillside site. In this sense, and despite its incongruous visual characteristics, the building is very much a product of its site.

In contrast to the internalized qualities of the gallery and theatre (where daylight is

gathered through roof lights rather than windows), the foyers open up behind glazing to read as a vast stage set viewed through the implied proscenium described by the rake of the roof and the falling ground-plane below; a great cavern that returns the activity of the building to the town – a powerful gesture set against the impervious nature of the tough metallic skin. Apart from some areas of glazing, aluminium is used everywhere for the external finish – shingles for the walls and linear sheeting on the roofs and roof lights. A staggered aluminium strip across the foyer's glass wall defines the presence of the stair and ramp behind. The foyer's openness effectively returns the ownership

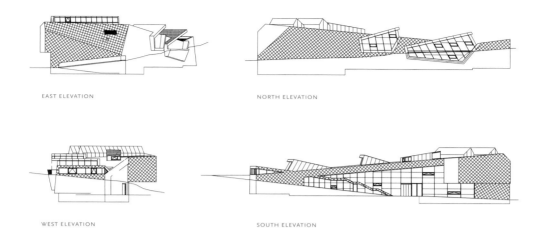

EAST ELEVATION   NORTH ELEVATION

WEST ELEVATION   SOUTH ELEVATION

0 ⌊_____⌋ 10

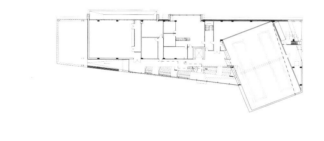

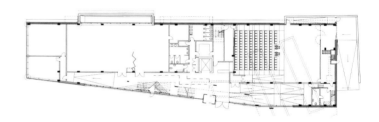

of the often esoteric world of the arts to the community from which it grows. The relationship of building to town through the foyer operates in both directions; the town sees the building as a living mechanism inviting inspection, and the foyer offers opportunities for the town to be viewed or re-viewed from the high level where two small terraces are cut into the roof plane creating semi-sheltered belvederes at either end. The building's abstract unconventional qualities are reinforced here.

Like the practice's Letterkenny Area Offices (p.140), this building consciously jars with the scale and built texture of the town.

Strangely, its somewhat crude and pragmatic qualities seem somehow appropriate and speak of a more significant connection with the region's landscape, and yet it is from further afield in central Europe that it draws it real inspiration. A project fitting for the edge of Europe.

AH

Grove Well-Being Centre

BELFAST
KENNEDY FITZGERALD & ASSOCIATES WITH AVANTI ARCHITECTS   2005–7

This project, due to be completed in 2007, combines the programmes for health-care and recreation within one superstructure sited in the Shore Road not far from the city centre but in an area that has little defining urban structure. Given the eroded nature of the urban context, the architects have looked to the landscape of Belfast's surrounding hills and mountains, a defining characteristic of the city frequently observed in the distance at the end of street views even from deep within the city centre.

The building is conceived as contributing to this topographical context by presenting itself as a single undulating hill-like form that acknowledges the slow curves of the distant skyline. To achieve this the roof is treated as a landscape out of which the architects have cut and described a series of terraces and courtyards that articulate the complexities of the building's multifarious uses. This topographical metaphor is not overworked – instead, the erosion of the roof plane provokes a different reading

of the building from street-level where it appears as a series of fingers that extend from a spine that runs parallel to the main frontage. At pavement level these fingers are gathered back together behind a continuous linear strip of steel mesh panelling through which courtyards may be viewed during the day whilst being back-lit with coloured illumination by night. Supergraphics applied to this panel emphasize the building's large scale and yet give it an abstract quality.

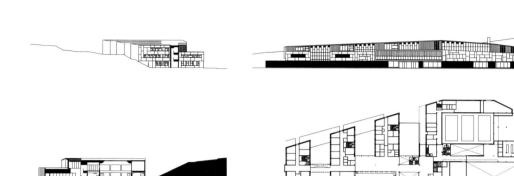

As with the Falls Leisure Centre (p.158) the regenerative potential of this project is significant in an area of the city that needs a strong landmark building. The plan form of the project, with its courtyard-like spaces, recalls the building style of some of the practice's earlier work such as Glenveagh School (p.108).

The last decade has given rise to a new architectural understanding of the extra large building as it emerges from the risible banality of the commercial shed. Belfast has seen a number of new buildings of this scale, none of which have managed to register against any significant architectural measure outside Northern Ireland. This project should do so and thereby raise architectural standards in a fast developing city in danger of succumbing to mediocrity.

AH

Monaghan County Council Offices

COMPETITION WINNING ENTRY
MONAGHAN   CO MONAGHAN
BOYD CODY ARCHITECTS   2005

This project, the winner of a competition in 2002, was planned to be built on the site of Monaghan's existing council offices. Whilst a portion of the existing building's concrete frame was to be responsibly retained, this was designed as a new building with a long plan which unravels to describe an angular figure across the site defining two south-facing courtyards. The defensive and institutional feeling of the existing building was intended to give way to one of openness and accessibility as the wooded site, in the suburbs of the town of Monaghan, fulfilled its nascent role as a civic forum presenting the new building clearly to the public across the more formal of the two courtyards.

The protracted plan form aims to evoke the experience of meandering through the site, allowing the building's occupants to feel close contact with the trees lining the perimeter. This sense of a close relationship to the site would give the building an informal quality appropriate for a contemporary government building and a generous use of space would characterize the circulation areas allowing staff and visitors alike to move easily through the building or along the sequential plan.

As with the internal circulation, it is intended that the public move in an informal way through a loosely defined foyer that permeates the ground floor as an unbroken

connection between the two entrance courts. The foyers have the quality of an abstracted landscape that nonetheless retains an ambience suitable for a public building. The radially configured council chamber, at first floor, would be seen over the more formal front entrance court through a long slot-window.

Despite the relaxed sense of informality that characterizes the plan, the intention was that the building would retain a distinctly civic appearance through a controlled palette of materials – glass, wood and stone. All external walls, bar the symbolically exposed chamber, were to be 'wrapped' in tall dignified timber louvres that operate

References

Boyd Cody Architects Dublin. In *10.10_2 : 100 architects, 10 critics*. London: Phaidon, 2005. 64-67.

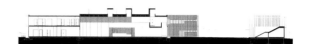

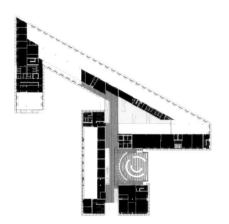

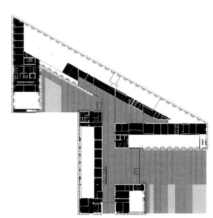

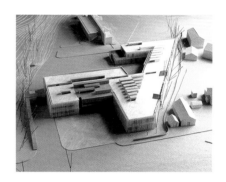

in a number of functional modes as they respond to differing external conditions – as brises-soleil to the south, east and west, and as a privacy screen for the nearby housing. To the north they would be least dense since coniferous trees line the nearby site boundary thereby obviating the need for privacy. Behind this wooden screen, the elements of the building would be gathered together as one legible whole. The array of linear roof lights dispersed over the building would give further expression of this complex but singular form. The roof lights, by admitting light from the south, east and west, would cause the building's internal character to change throughout the day and across the

seasons thus creating a further connection with the site.

Charged with a kind of robust dignity, this building has found a language for its modest suburban location that demonstrates humane and democratic architecture whilst conceding none of its civic credentials. It is to be hoped that the project will eventually be built.

AH

Lyric Theatre

COMPETION WINNING ENTRY
BELFAST
O'DONNELL & TUOMEY   2003

This project was the winning entry in an international design competition held in 2003. Whilst other entries proposed more autonomous buildings, this one is anchored to its context, recognising the character of the surrounding streetscape with the adoption of red brick as the prevailing material. Fundamental to Belfast's urban character, the brick is drawn from the street into the building's foyers behind a vast glazed screen. Here, the presence of the auditorium (again, made from red brick) seems to complete or conclude the terrace from which it apparently grows – a shift from domestic to civic through the continuous use of

one material. Yet despite this continuity the auditorium can still be read as a distinct entity (embedded but identifiable) as the modest scale of the street gives way to a larger, more abstract language. This 'revealed' quality of the auditorium-form could be compared to the traditional 'encapsulation' of auditoria observed in Beaux-Arts examples where, predominantly, the internal form is only experienced after passing through a more dense and compact plan arrangement. By contrast, this project expresses its constituent parts as though the theatre has been opened or unwrapped to reveal itself both philosophically and literally to the city. It

could be said that the openness of this gesture reflects the creative ethos of the Lyric Theatre Company itself.

The plan directly describes the influx of visitors to the theatre as they move along the nearby streets and riverside into the foyers and up to galleries offering views back over the river. The ascent works its way around the rear of the auditorium giving further definition to it as a distinct space, room or destination. The auditorium is entered at the highest level from where the audience make their way down either side of one singular raked body of seating that gathers the audience

References

McCloskey, F. A theatrical experience. *Perspective*, 12(6), 2003. 47-49.

A house for the Lyric: competition for the Lyric Theatre, Belfast. *Architecture Ireland*, (194), 2004. 59.

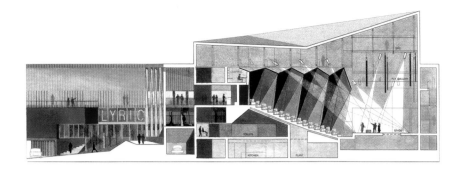
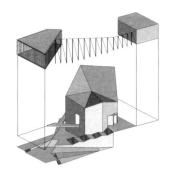

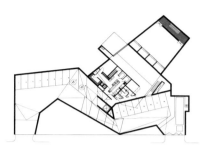

BASEMENT FLOOR

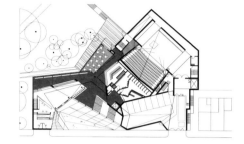

GROUND FLOOR

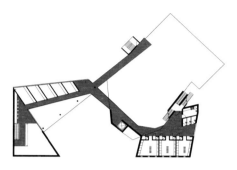

MEZZANINE FLOOR

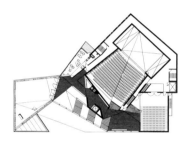

FIRST FLOOR

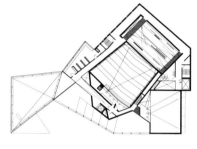

SECOND FLOOR

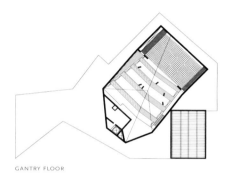

GANTRY FLOOR

together in one mass thereby creating a very direct and powerful relationship with the performers and stage.

In addition to their use of brickwork, the architects delicately enclose the foyer spaces and rehearsal room with lighter, glazed skins – transparent to the foyer but translucent to the rehearsal space (which, when lit within at night, becomes a beacon or lantern to the river basin and its environs). The dominant high corner position allotted to the rehearsal space asserts the significance of the day-to-day activities of the theatre – in this way the tradition of 'back-of-house' becomes subverted.

The project eschews any ideas of fashionable architectural beauty in favour of a tough, almost pragmatic quality that reflects the honest unpretentious character of the city itself. This project's unwrapped 'lain bare' nature speaks of the theatre's civic purpose whilst describing a more contemporary sense of social responsibility.

AH

Giant's Causeway Visitors' Centre

COMPETITION WINNING ENTRY
BUSHMILLS   CO ANTRIM
HENEGHAN PENG ARCHITECTS   2005

Heneghan Peng had already established a reputation as competition winners before the Giant's Causeway competition where they came first in an international field of some 200 entries. Earlier successes include the 2001 competition for the combined civic offices of Kildare County Council and Naas Town Council, and the Carlisle pier development in Dun Laoghaire in 2004 when their short-listed rivals included Skidmore Owings and Merrill, Daniel Libeskind and Scott Tallon Walker. Their major success, however, came in 2003 in winning the competition for the Grand Museum for Egypt in Cairo. Roisin Heneghan studied architecture at University College Dublin before moving to the Graduate School at Harvard where

she met Shih-Fu Peng. They graduated in 1992 and set up practice together in 1999. In 2001 they relocated to Dublin.

The Causeway project is modest in scale when compared to the Egyptian competition which attracted a field of over 1,500 entries but it also occupies a World Heritage site and it, too, reveals a mastery in the handling of site and landscape. In the words of the jury the entry, 'exudes a simple and quiet monumentality that evokes a strong sense of drama and expectation'. In this gesture of monumental minimalism, the terrain is sculpted to house the visitors' centre beneath the lie of the land and leave the ridge line at the approach to the Causeway unbroken. No new structures

rise above this line and the Centre is housed in the planes of the landscape; its edge defined by angular planes of glazing which rise and fall along the perimeter. Car parking is situated in a recessed forecourt from where a gentle grass-covered ramp leads the visitor to the top of the ridge and a first view of the Causeway beyond. A short tunnel at the corner of the car park passes through the ridge and connects it to the road to the Causeway.

The seven-man jury was chaired by the eminent Finnish architect and theorist Juhani Pallasmaa and his enthusiasm for the scheme is evident in the jury's report which commented, 'the design responded to the elemental power within

References

Girvan, W. D. Survey and list of historical buildings: North Antrim. Belfast: UAHS, 1972.

McCloskey, F. Folds in the landscape: visitors' centre for the Giant's Causeway. Perspective,14(6), 2005. 18-21.

Architectural assessment: report of the jury to the project promoter. Belfast: unpublished document, 2005.

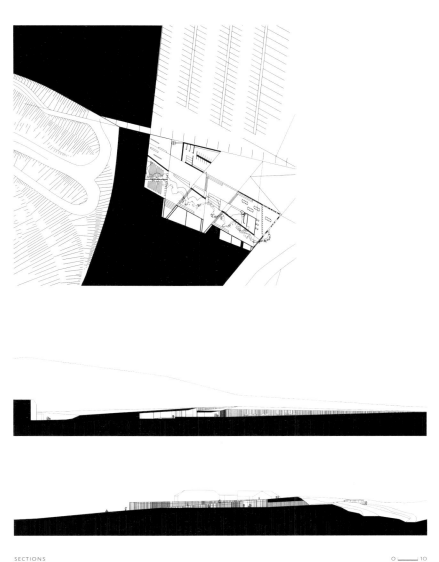

SECTIONS   0 ⌐——⌐ 10

the geological formation of the site with scale and grandeur'. However, in a note of caution, the report commented that the 'function of the grass roof with glazed walls was crucial' and that 'the unavoidable thickness of the grass roof as well as the obligatory railings or balustrades would have to be rigorously resolved'. The design proposed no further buildings on the site and the 'visual power of the cuts and slopes mediated between the [existing] structures to create a unity'. These three buildings consist of the Causeway Hotel, a small Tudor-style school house of the 19th century and Clough Williams Ellis's Giant's Causeway Church of Ireland school with a tiled and louvred bell-tower 'reminiscent of an

Austrian village church'. The building, in the words of the author of the UAHS's North Antrim list, 'seems to take a light-hearted attitude to the grandeur of the surrounding scenery'.

Over the centuries the Giant's Causeway has been a source of marvel and wonder to travellers, and the Romantics of the late-18th century thrilled to the wild grandeur of the scene. Dr Johnson felt that although the Causeway was worth seeing it was 'not worth going to see'. The 19th century took a different view and it became the greatest attraction for visitors to Antrim. In 1883 a narrow gauge railway was built to the Causeway, the world's first hydroelectric tramway designed by

Colonel William Traill which wound its way along the coastline from Portrush. It closed in 1949. Since then the Visitors' Centre designed by Bergin Associates and occupying the present site provided a focus for visitors. It burnt down in 2000. This new proposal marks yet another response to our national treasure and it takes a wholly responsive attitude to the surrounding scenery. If Dr Johnson were to take a return trip in the future he may consider the journey worthwhile.

DE

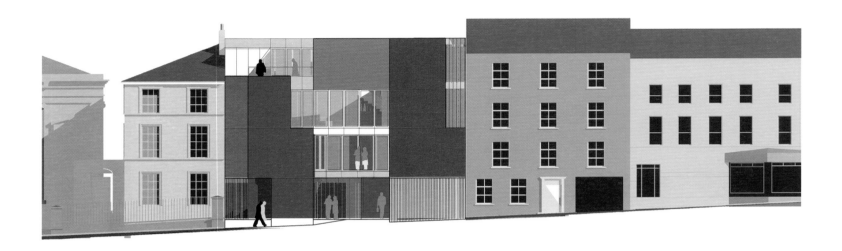

An Gaeláras

COMPETITION WINNING ENTRY
DERRY   CO LONDONDERRY
O'DONNELL & TUOMEY   2004

This project, for an Irish Language Centre, was won through competition in 2004 and is due to commence on site in 2006. The project followed shortly after the practice's commission for the Lyric Theatre (another winning competition entry featured on p.174) and similarly explores the idea of urban landscape extending within a building to create a rich compact collection of spaces.

In this case, the building is sited adjacent to a church and within a well-established urban block. Rather than reassert the reading of the block as a solid object through a conventional façade, the elevation of this building breaks apart and fragments into pieces thereby giving the street a more open quality. Between these pieces, the landscape of the street finds its way informally into the building. Rather than circulation being based on an orthogonal geometry, the angular patterns of the plan encourage exploration deep into the site toward the top-lit courtyard space in the centre of the plot. On a site where only one of the elevations can be fenestrated, the roof is employed as a second elevation to draw light deep down into the ground floor.

The building may be considered to be an agglomeration of pieces including the residual space around and between them. Their position, relative to each other, has become so compressed that they reappear as one contiguous cluster. In terms of this density, the building is analogous to the city itself – compact and varied – a world where small spaces evoke timeless urban values despite modest physical dimensions.

AH

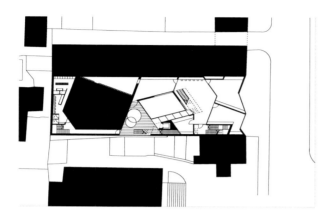

SECOND FLOOR

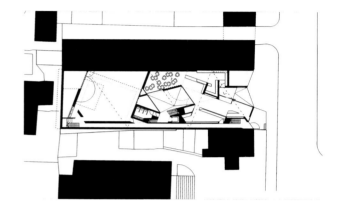

GROUND FLOOR

SECTIONS

RESOURCES

PICTURE CREDITS

The authors and publishers wish to thank the individuals and institutions who have provided drawings and photographic material for use in this book and granted permission to reproduce them. Every effort has been made to trace and contact the copyright holders before publication but, if notified, the publisher will rectify any inadvertent errors or omissions at the earliest opportunity. In most cases the drawings for the individual building studies were provided by the architects for the project. The credits for all the photographs illustrating the essays in Part One are listed on the appropriate pages. Photographs 1.23, 1.24, 1.30 and 1.43 are reproduced with the kind permission of the Trustees of the National Museums Northern Ireland. The photographs in Part Two were taken by Mark Hackett apart from the following:

Paddy Acheson p.108 (left & top right)

Robert J Anderson & Anderson McMeekin p.54 (top left), p.55(top), p.78, p.96-7, p.98, p.126, p.127(centre)

Architectural Press Archive / RIBA Library Photographs Collection p.68 (right)

Crispin Boyle / RIBA Library Photographs Collection p.99

Ian Campbell p.54 (bottom), p.100

WD Fry p.55 (bottom)

Alastair Hall p.117, p.119 (top left, bottom)

Chris Hill p.103 (left), p.110, p.116, p.118, p.119 (top right), p.120, p.121, p.142, p.143 (left)

Michael Hutchinson p.128-9

Norman Hutchinson p.108 (bottom right), p.109, p.158-9

Alan Jones p.156-7

Ros Kavanagh p.148-9

Paul Larmour p.50 (left), p.51 (left), p.52 (bottom left), p.53 (right), p.54 (left), p.60 (right), p.61 (2nd left), p.62-3, p.82 (right), p.83, p.84, p.88, p.89 (top right & middle), p.90 (bottom), p.92 (top, bottom left & right), p.93, p.94 (left & middle), p.95

Gareth Maguire p.76, p.87 (top), p.102, p.103 (right)

Paul Megahey p.162-3

RSUA Yearbook p.87 (bottom)

Todd Watson p.131, p.138, p.139 (right), p.146-7, p.152 (right), p.153 (middle), p.160-1

Sean Watters p.54 (top right), p.89 (top left & bottom), p.90 (top left & right)

Charlotte Wood p.114.

Detailed references to specific buildings referred to in the text are found appended to the essays and the relevant building entries.

Surveys of Modern Ulster Architecture

Architecture in Britain today. 4: Northern Ireland. *RIBA Journal*, 85(8), 1978. 334-39.

Becker, A., Olley, J. and Wang, W. (eds). *20th century architecture: Ireland.* New York and Munich: Prestel Verlag, 1997.

Dixon, H. *An introduction to Ulster architecture.* Belfast: UAHS, 1975.

Evans, D. *An introduction to modern Ulster architecture.* Belfast: UAHS, 1977.

Larmour, P. *Belfast: an illustrated architectural guide.* Belfast: Friar's Bush Press, 1987.

Larmour, P. *Festival of architecture 1834-1984.* Belfast: RSUA, 1984.

Larmour, P. International exposure for Ulster architecture. *Perspective*, 6(2), 1997. 62-66.

Larmour, P. Post-war listings in Northern Ireland. *Perspective*, 15(1), 2006. 40-48.

Larmour, P. and Evans, D. Northern Ireland: architecture. In Turner, J.S. (ed). *The dictionary of art.* v.16. London: Macmillan, 1996. 39-40.

McKinstry, R. Contemporary architecture. In Longley, M. (ed). *Causeway: the arts in Ulster.* Belfast: Arts Council of Northern Ireland, 1971. 27-42.

McKinstry, R. Life and work today for the architect in Ulster. *Architects' Journal*, 113(2935),1951. 697-712.

Rothery, S. *Ireland and the new architecture 1900-1940.* Dublin: Lilliput Press, 1991.

General and Comparative Works

Colquhoun, A. *Modern architecture.* Oxford: Oxford University Press, 2002.

Curtis, W. *Modern architecture since 1900.* 3rd ed. London: Phaidon, 1996.

Dannat, T. *Modern architecture in Britain.* London: Batsford, 1959.

Frampton, K. *Modern architecture: a critical history.* London: Thames and Hudson, 1980.

Graby, J. (ed). *Building on the edge of Europe.* Dublin: RIAI, 1996.

Jencks, C. *Modern movements in architecture.* London: Penguin Books, 1987.

Lampugnani, V.L. (ed). *Dictionary of 20th century architecture.* London: Thames and Hudson, 1996.

Moffett, N. *The best of British architecture, 1980 to 2000.* London: Spon, 1993.

Powers, A. *Modern: the Modern Movement in Britain.* London: Merrell, 2005.

Sharp: D. *Twentieth century architecture: a visual history.* London: Lund Humphries, 1991.

Contemporary Buildings

The following periodicals and annuals published in Ireland have featured prominent late twentieth century buildings in Ulster as they have appeared, as well as some historical articles on architects who have contributed to the development of Modernism in Ulster.

Architecture Ireland. Dublin: RIAI. 2003- (formerly *Irish Architect* and *Bulletin of the RIAI*)

Irish Architectural Review. Dublin: RIAI. 1999-

New Irish Architecture: AAI awards. Dublin: Architectural Association of Ireland. 1986-

Perspective. Belfast: Royal Society of Ulster Architects. 1992-

Plan. Dublin. 1969-

Ulster Architect. Belfast. 1984-

Further Information

PADDI: *Planning Architecture Design Database Ireland*

PADDI is a freely available online database (www.paddi.net) which contains thousands of records indexing information on all aspects of architecture and planning in Ireland. As well as listing references to information in books, articles, reports and theses, PADDI also provides a directory to the major architectural collections in Ireland.